FIVB™

排球竞赛规则
OFFICIAL VOLLEYBALL RULES
2021—2024

国际排联2021年第37届代表大会通过

中国排球协会　译定

人民体育出版社

图书在版编目（CIP）数据

排球竞赛规则 . 2021—2024 / 中国排球协会译定
. -- 北京 : 人民体育出版社 , 2023
ISBN 978-7-5009-6254-0

Ⅰ . ①排… Ⅱ . ①中… Ⅲ . ①排球运动—竞赛规则—2021-2024 Ⅳ . ① G842.4

中国版本图书馆 CIP 数据核字 (2022) 第 247881 号

*

人 民 体 育 出 版 社 出 版 发 行
北 京 中 科 印 刷 有 限 公 司 印 刷
新 华 书 店 经 销

*

880 × 1230　32 开本　6.875 印张　200 千字
2023 年 4 月第 1 版　2023 年 4 月第 1 次印刷

*

ISBN 978-7-5009-6254-0
定价：38.00 元

社址：北京市东城区体育馆路 8 号（天坛公园东门）
电话：67151482（发行部）　　邮编：100061
传真：67151483　　邮购：67118491
网址：www.psphpress.com
（购买本社图书，如遇有缺损页可与邮购部联系）

说　明

国际排球联合会于2021年第37届代表大会通过的这本《排球竞赛规则2021—2024》（以下简称本《规则》），经中国排球协会译定，在全国各级排球比赛中执行。条款中用黑体字排印的词语和段落，是重点强调以及在"国际排联比赛、世界性比赛和正式比赛"中必须执行的规定。

为提高排球工作者的英语水平和便于国际交流，本《规则》改进了以往的排版方式，使用了更加方便阅读的中英文对照排版。

本《规则》在翻译、校订和整理过程中，得到了本协会裁判委员会的大力协助，在此特别致谢。

中国排球协会
2021年7月

目　录

CONTENTS

GAME CHARACTERISTICS 01

PART 1 PHILOSOPHY OF RULES AND REFEREEING 02

PART 2 SECTION 1: GAME 08

CHAPTER 1 FACILITIES AND EQUIPMENT 10

1 PLAYING AREA ········ 10
1.1 DIMENSIONS ········ 10
1.2 PLAYING SURFACE ········ 10
1.3 LINES ON THE COURT ········ 12
1.4 ZONES AND AREAS ········ 14
1.5 TEMPERATURE ········ 16
1.6 LIGHTING ········ 16
2 NET AND POSTS ········ 16
2.1 HEIGHT OF THE NET ········ 16
2.2 STRUCTURE ········ 18
2.3 SIDE BANDS ········ 18
2.4 ANTENNAE ········ 20
2.5 POSTS ········ 20
2.6 ADDITIONAL EQUIPMENT ········ 20
3 BALLS ········ 22
3.1 STANDARDS ········ 22
3.2 UNIFORMITY OF BALLS ········ 22
3.3 BALL RETRIEVAL SYSTEM ········ 22

CHAPTER 2 PARTICIPANTS 24

4 TEAMS ········ 24
4.1 TEAM COMPOSITION ········ 24
4.2 LOCATION OF THE TEAM ········ 26
4.3 EQUIPMENT ········ 28
4.4 CHANGE OF EQUIPMENT ········ 30
4.5 FORBIDDEN OBJECTS ········ 30

比赛的特性 01

第一部分 规则与裁判工作的指导思想 03

第二部分 第一章：比赛 09

第一节 器材与设备 11

1 比赛场地……11
  1.1 面积……11
  1.2 比赛场地地面……11
  1.3 场地上的画线……13
  1.4 区与区域……15
  1.5 温度……17
  1.6 照明……17
2 球网与网柱……17
  2.1 球网高度……17
  2.2 构造……19
  2.3 标志带……19
  2.4 标志杆……21
  2.5 网柱……21
  2.6 附加设备……21
3 球……23
  3.1 标准……23
  3.2 统一性……23
  3.3 5 球制……23

第二节 比赛参加者 25

4 比赛队……25
  4.1 队的组成……25
  4.2 队的位置……27
  4.3 装备……29
  4.4 服装的更换……31
  4.5 禁止佩戴的物品……31

5 TEAM LEADERS ········ 30
5.1 CAPTAIN ········ 32
5.2 COACH ········ 34
5.3 ASSISTANT COACH ········ 36

CHAPTER 3 PLAYING FORMAT 38

6 TO SCORE A POINT, TO WIN A SET AND THE MATCH ········ 38
6.1 TO SCORE A POINT ········ 38
6.2 TO WIN A SET ········ 40
6.3 TO WIN THE MATCH ········ 40
6.4 DEFAULT AND INCOMPLETE TEAM ········ 40
7 STRUCTURE OF PLAY ········ 42
7.1 THE TOSS ········ 42
7.2 OFFICIAL WARM-UP SESSION ········ 44
7.3 TEAM STARTING LINE-UP ········ 44
7.4 POSITIONS ········ 48
7.5 POSITIONAL FAULT ········ 50
7.6 ROTATION ········ 50
7.7 ROTATIONAL FAULT ········ 52

CHAPTER 4 PLAYING ACTIONS 54

8 STATES OF PLAY ········ 54
8.1 BALL IN PLAY ········ 54
8.2 BALL OUT OF PLAY ········ 54
8.3 BALL "IN" ········ 54
8.4 BALL "OUT" ········ 54
9 PLAYING THE BALL ········ 56
9.1 TEAM HITS ········ 56
9.2 CHARACTERISTICS OF THE HIT ········ 58
9.3 FAULTS IN PLAYING THE BALL ········ 60
10 BALL AT THE NET ········ 60
10.1 BALL CROSSING THE NET ········ 60
10.2 BALL TOUCHING THE NET ········ 62
10.3 BALL IN THE NET ········ 62

5 队的领导…31
5.1 队长…33
5.2 教练员…35
5.3 助理教练员…37

第三节 比赛方法 39

6 得1分、胜1局与胜1场…39
6.1 得1分…39
6.2 胜1局…41
6.3 胜1场…41
6.4 弃权与阵容不完整…41
7 比赛的组织…43
7.1 抽签…43
7.2 准备活动…45
7.3 球队首发阵容…45
7.4 位置…49
7.5 位置错误…51
7.6 轮转…51
7.7 轮转错误…53

第四节 比赛行为 55

8 比赛的状态…55
8.1 进入比赛…55
8.2 比赛的中止…55
8.3 界内球…55
8.4 界外球…55
9 击球…57
9.1 球队的击球…57
9.2 击球的性质…59
9.3 击球时的犯规…61
10 球网附近的球…61
10.1 球通过球网…61
10.2 球触球网…63
10.3 球入球网…63

11 PLAYER AT THE NET ········ 62
11.1 REACHING BEYOND THE NET ········ 62
11.2 PENETRATION UNDER THE NET ········ 62
11.3 CONTACT WITH THE NET ········ 64
11.4 PLAYER'S FAULTS AT THE NET ········ 66
12 SERVICE ········ 66
12.1 FIRST SERVICE IN A SET ········ 68
12.2 SERVICE ORDER ········ 68
12.3 AUTHORIZATION OF THE SERVICE ········ 68
12.4 EXECUTION OF THE SERVICE ········ 68
12.5 SCREENING ········ 70
12.6 FAULTS MADE DURING THE SERVICE ········ 70
12.7 SERVING FAULTS AND POSITIONAL FAULTS ········ 72
13 ATTACK HIT ········ 72
13.1 CHARACTERISTICS OF THE ATTACK HIT ········ 72
13.2 RESTRICTIONS OF THE ATTACK HIT ········ 74
13.3 FAULTS OF THE ATTACK HIT ········ 74
14 BLOCK ········ 76
14.1 BLOCKING ········ 76
14.2 BLOCK CONTACT ········ 78
14.3 BLOCKING WITHIN THE OPPONENT'S SPACE ········ 78
14.4 BLOCK AND TEAM HITS ········ 78
14.5 BLOCKING THE SERVICE ········ 78
14.6 BLOCKING FAULTS ········ 78

CHAPTER 5 INTERRUPTIONS, DELAYS AND INTERVALS 82

15 INTERRUPTIONS ········ 82
15.1 NUMBER OF REGULAR GAME INTERRUPTIONS ········ 82
15.2 SEQUENCE OF REGULAR GAME INTERRUPTIONS ········ 82
15.3 REQUEST FOR REGULAR GAME INTERRUPTIONS ········ 84
15.4 TIME-OUTS ········ 84
15.5 SUBSTITUTION ········ 84
15.6 LIMITATION OF SUBSTITUTIONS ········ 86
15.7 EXCEPTIONAL SUBSTITUTION ········ 86

11 球网附近的队员……63
11.1 越过球网……63
11.2 网下穿越……63
11.3 触网……65
11.4 队员在球网附近的犯规……67
12 发球……67
12.1 首先发球……69
12.2 发球的次序……69
12.3 发球的允许……69
12.4 发球的执行……69
12.5 发球掩护……71
12.6 发球时的犯规……71
12.7 发球犯规与位置错误……73
13 进攻性击球……73
13.1 进攻性击球的特性……73
13.2 进攻性击球的限制……75
13.3 进攻性击球的犯规……75
14 拦网……77
14.1 拦网行为……77
14.2 拦网触球……79
14.3 在对方空间内拦网……79
14.4 拦网与球队的击球……79
14.5 拦发球……79
14.6 拦网犯规……79

第五节 比赛间断与延误比赛 83

15 间断……83
15.1 合法比赛间断的次数……83
15.2 合法比赛间断的次序……83
15.3 请求合法比赛间断……85
15.4 暂停……85
15.5 换人……85
15.6 换人的限制……87
15.7 特殊换人……87

15.8 SUBSTITUTION FOR EXPULSION OR DISQUALIFICATION ········ 88
15.9 ILLEGAL SUBSTITUTION ········ 88
15.10 SUBSTITUTION PROCEDURE ········ 88
15.11 IMPROPER REQUESTS ········ 90
16 GAME DELAYS ········ 92
16.1 TYPES OF DELAYS ········ 92
16.2 DELAY SANCTIONS ········ 94
17 EXCEPTIONAL GAME INTERRUPTIONS ········ 94
17.1 INJURY/ ILLNESS ········ 94
17.2 EXTERNAL INTERFERENCE ········ 96
17.3 PROLONGED INTERRUPTIONS ········ 96
18 INTERVALS AND CHANGE OF COURTS ········ 96
18.1 INTERVALS ········ 96
18.2 CHANGE OF COURTS ········ 98

CHAPTER 6 THE LIBERO PLAYER 100

19 THE LIBERO PLAYER ········ 100
19.1 DESIGNATION OF THE LIBERO ········ 100
19.2 EQUIPMENT ········ 100
19.3 ACTIONS INVOLVING THE LIBERO ········ 102
19.4 RE-DESIGNATION OF A NEW LIBERO ········ 106
19.5 SUMMARY ········ 108

CHAPTER 7 PARTICIPANTS' CONDUCT 110

20 REQUIREMENTS OF CONDUCT ········ 110
20.1 SPORTSMANLIKE CONDUCT ········ 110
20.2 FAIR PLAY ········ 110
21 MISCONDUCT AND ITS SANCTIONS ········ 112
21.1 MINOR MISCONDUCT ········ 112
21.2 MISCONDUCT LEADING TO SANCTIONS ········ 112
21.3 SANCTION SCALE ········ 114
21.4 APPLICATION OF MISCONDUCT SANCTIONS ········ 116
21.5 MISCONDUCT BEFORE AND BETWEEN SETS ········ 116
21.6 SUMMARY OF MISCONDUCT AND CARDS USED ········ 116

15.8 被判罚出场或被取消比赛资格的换人 …… 89
15.9 不合法的换人 …… 89
15.10 换人的程序 …… 89
15.11 不符合规定的请求 …… 91
16 延误比赛 …… 93
16.1 延误比赛的类型 …… 93
16.2 对延误比赛的处罚 …… 95
17 例外的比赛中断 …… 95
17.1 受伤或生病 …… 95
17.2 外因造成的比赛中断 …… 97
17.3 被拖延的间断 …… 97
18 局间休息与交换场区 …… 97
18.1 局间休息 …… 97
18.2 交换场区 …… 99

第六节 自由防守队员 101

19 自由防守队员 …… 101
19.1 自由防守队员的指定 …… 101
19.2 装备 …… 101
19.3 自由防守队员涉及的行为 …… 103
19.4 指定新自由防守队员 …… 107
19.5 概要 …… 109

第七节 参赛者的行为 111

20 行为要求 …… 111
20.1 体育道德 …… 111
20.2 公正竞赛 …… 111
21 不良行为及其处罚 …… 113
21.1 轻微的不良行为 …… 113
21.2 给予处罚的不良行为 …… 113
21.3 处罚等级 …… 115
21.4 处罚的实施 …… 117
21.5 局前与局间的不良行为 …… 117
21.6 不良行为的种类与红黄牌的使用 …… 117

PART 2 SECTION 2: THE REFEREES, THEIR RESPONSIBILITIES AND OFFICIAL HAND SIGNALS 120

CHAPTER 8 REFEREES 122

22 REFEREEING TEAM AND PROCEDURES 122
22.1 COMPOSITION 122
22.2 PROCEDURES 122
23 1st REFEREE 126
23.1 LOCATION 126
23.2 AUTHORITY 126
23.3 RESPONSIBILITIES 128
24 2nd REFEREE 130
24.1 LOCATION 130
24.2 AUTHORITY 132
24.3 RESPONSIBILITIES 134
25 CHALLENGE REFEREE 136
25.1 LOCATION 136
25.2 RESPONSIBILITIES 136
26 RESERVE REFEREE 136
26.1 LOCATION 136
26.2 RESPONSIBILITIES 138
27 SCORER 138
27.1 LOCATION 138
27.2 RESPONSIBILITIES 140
28 ASSISTANT SCORER 142
28.1 LOCATION 142
28.2 RESPONSIBILITIES 142
29 LINE JUDGES 146
29.1 LOCATION 146
29.2 RESPONSIBILITIES 146
30 OFFICIAL SIGNALS 148
30.1 REFEREES' HAND SIGNALS 148
30.2 LINE JUDGES' FLAG SIGNALS 148

第二部分 第二章：裁判员及其职责与法定手势 121

第八节 裁判员 123

22 裁判团队与工作程序……123
22.1 组成……123
22.2 工作程序……123
23 第 1 裁判员……127
23.1 位置……127
23.2 权力……127
23.3 职责……129
24 第 2 裁判员……131
24.1 位置……131
24.2 权力……133
24.3 职责……135
25 挑战裁判员……137
25.1 位置……137
25.2 职责……137
26 替补裁判员……137
26.1 位置……137
26.2 职责……139
27 记录员……139
27. 1 位置……139
27.2 职责……141
28 辅助记录员……143
28.1 位置……143
28.2 职责……143
29 司线员……147
29.1 位置……147
29.2 职责……147
30 法定手势……149
30.1 裁判员的手势……149
30.2 司线员的旗示……149

PART 2 SECTION 3: DIAGRAMS 150

DIAGRAM 1a: COMPETITION / CONTROL AREA ········ 152
DIAGRAM 1b: THE PLAYING AREA ········ 154
DIAGRAM 2: THE PLAYING COURT ········ 156
DIAGRAM 3: DESIGN OF THE NET ········ 158
DIAGRAM 4: POSITION OF PLAYERS ········ 160
DIAGRAM 5a: BALL CROSSING THE VERTICAL PLANE OF THE NET TO THE OPPONENT COURT ··· 162
DIAGRAM 5b: BALL CROSSING THE VERTICAL PLANE OF THE NET TO THE OPPONENT FREE ZONE ··· 164
DIAGRAM 6: COLLECTIVE SCREEN ········ 166
DIAGRAM 7: COMPLETED BLOCK ········ 166
DIAGRAM 8: BACK ROW PLAYER'S ATTACK ········ 168
DIAGRAM 9: WARNINGS AND SANCTIONS SCALES AND THEIR CONSEQUENCES ······ 170
9a: MISCONDUCT WARNINGS AND SANCTIONS ········ 170
9b: DELAY WARNING SYMBOLS AND SANCTIONS ········ 170
DIAGRAM 10: LOCATION OF REFEREEING TEAM AND THEIR ASSISTANTS ········ 172
DIAGRAM 11: REFEREES' OFFICIAL HAND SIGNALS ········ 174
DIAGRAM 12: LINE JUDGES' OFFICIAL FLAG SIGNALS ········ 188

PART 3 DEFINITIONS 192

第二部分：第三章　图表　151

图 1a：竞赛控制区…………153
图 1b：比赛场地…………155
图 2：比赛场区…………157
图 3：球网的规格…………159
图 4：队员的位置…………161
图 5a：球通过球网垂直平面进入对方场区…………163
图 5b：球通过球网垂直平面进入对方无障碍区…………165
图 6：发球时的集体掩护…………167
图 7：完成拦网…………167
图 8：后排队员进攻性击球…………169
图 9：警告和处罚等级表及其后续结果…………171
9a：不良行为的警告和处罚…………171
9b：延误处罚等级表…………171
图 10: 裁判员与辅助人员位置…………173
图 11：裁判员手势…………175
图 12：司线员旗示…………189

第三部分　定义　193

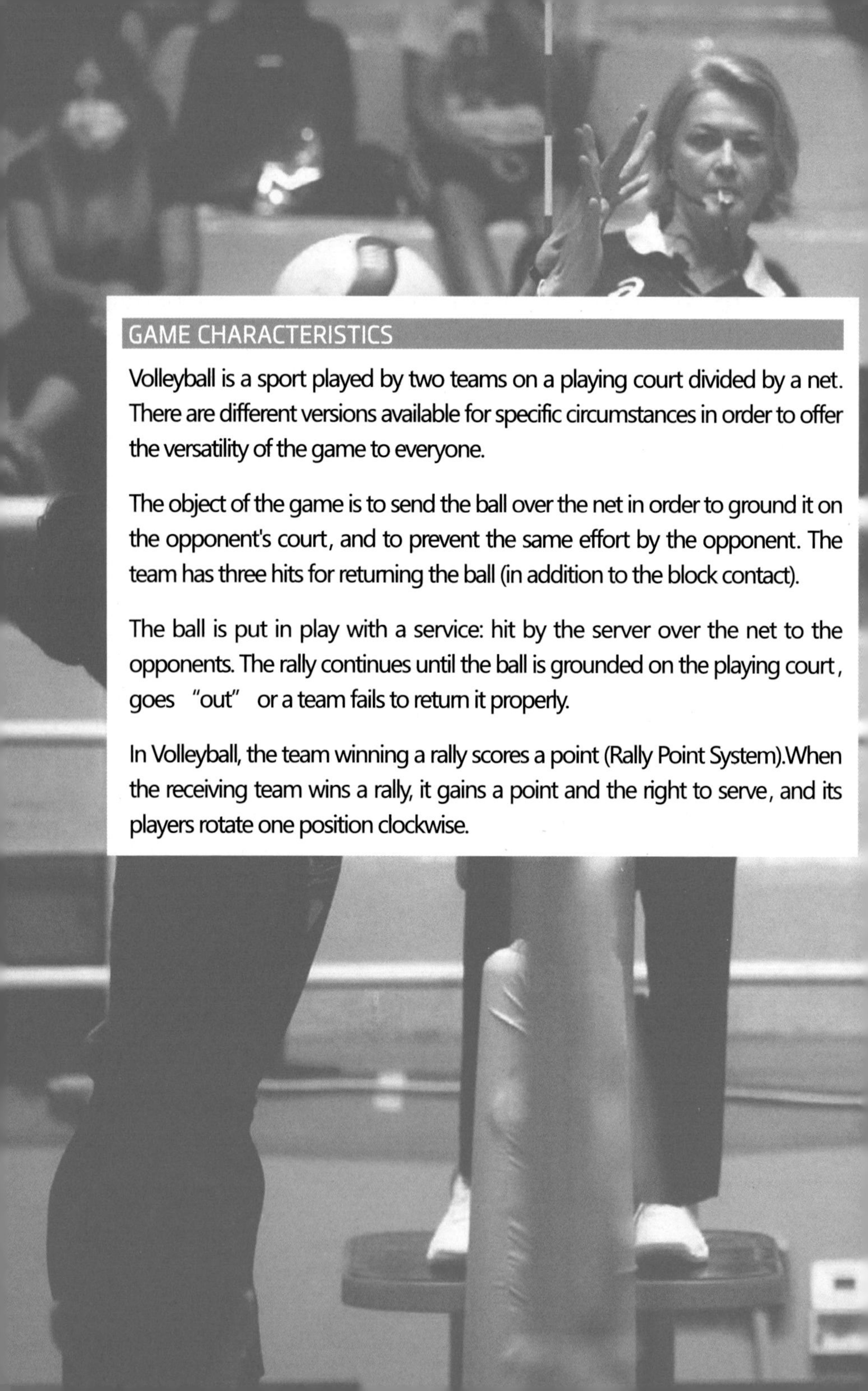

GAME CHARACTERISTICS

Volleyball is a sport played by two teams on a playing court divided by a net. There are different versions available for specific circumstances in order to offer the versatility of the game to everyone.

The object of the game is to send the ball over the net in order to ground it on the opponent's court, and to prevent the same effort by the opponent. The team has three hits for returning the ball (in addition to the block contact).

The ball is put in play with a service: hit by the server over the net to the opponents. The rally continues until the ball is grounded on the playing court, goes "out" or a team fails to return it properly.

In Volleyball, the team winning a rally scores a point (Rally Point System).When the receiving team wins a rally, it gains a point and the right to serve, and its players rotate one position clockwise.

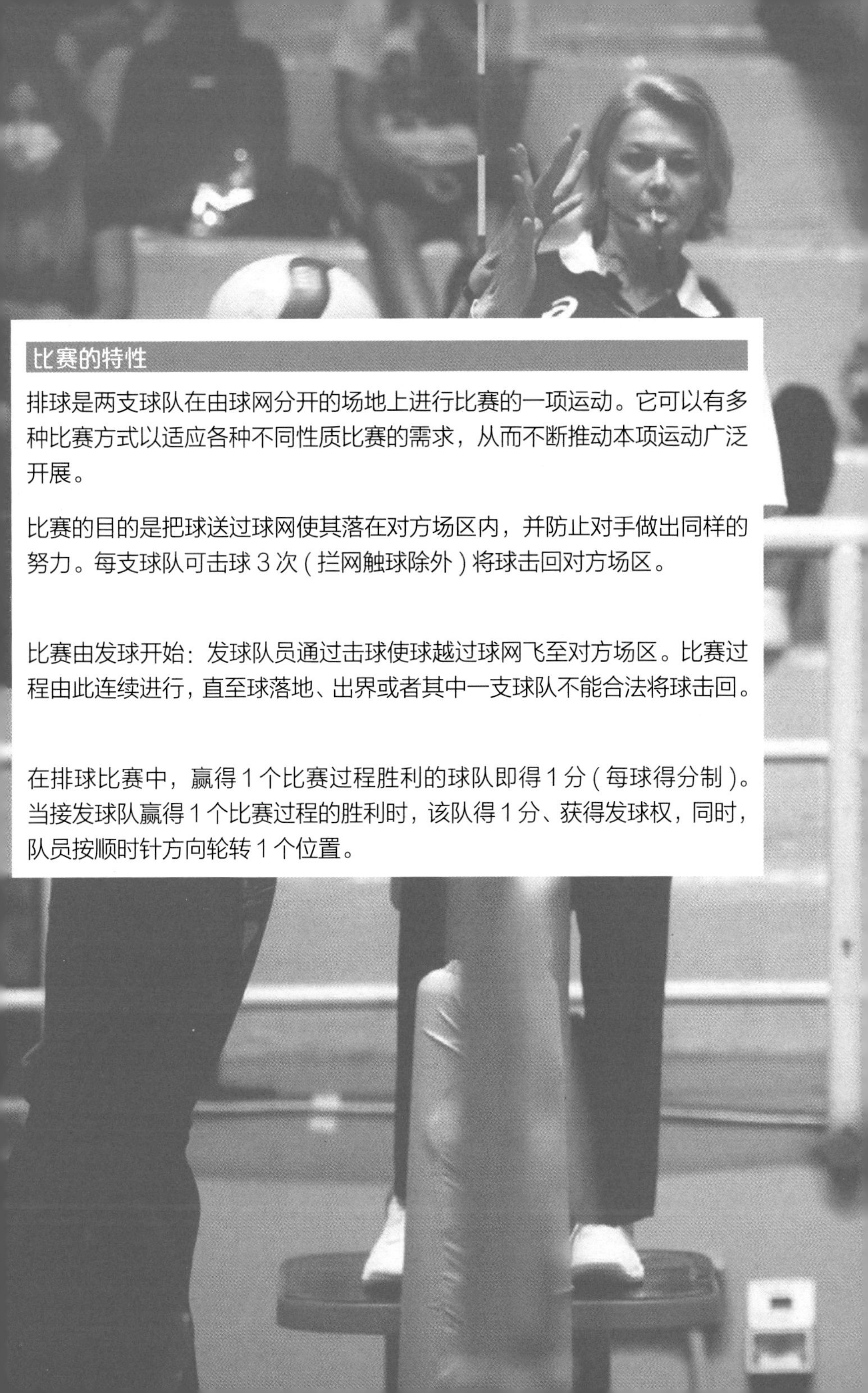

比赛的特性

排球是两支球队在由球网分开的场地上进行比赛的一项运动。它可以有多种比赛方式以适应各种不同性质比赛的需求，从而不断推动本项运动广泛开展。

比赛的目的是把球送过球网使其落在对方场区内，并防止对手做出同样的努力。每支球队可击球 3 次 (拦网触球除外) 将球击回对方场区。

比赛由发球开始：发球队员通过击球使球越过球网飞至对方场区。比赛过程由此连续进行，直至球落地、出界或者其中一支球队不能合法将球击回。

在排球比赛中，赢得 1 个比赛过程胜利的球队即得 1 分 (每球得分制)。当接发球队赢得 1 个比赛过程的胜利时，该队得 1 分、获得发球权，同时，队员按顺时针方向轮转 1 个位置。

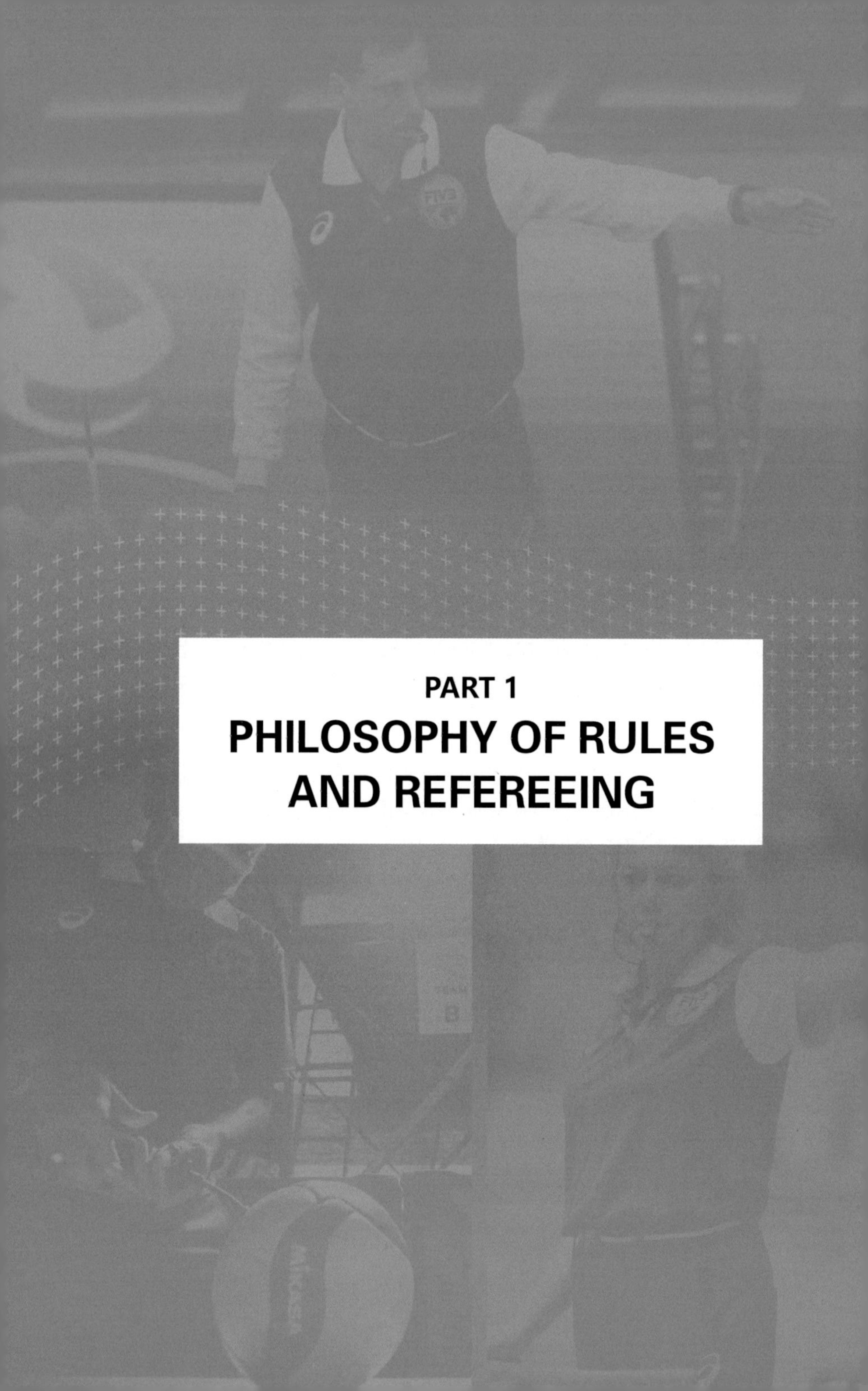

PART 1
PHILOSOPHY OF RULES AND REFEREEING

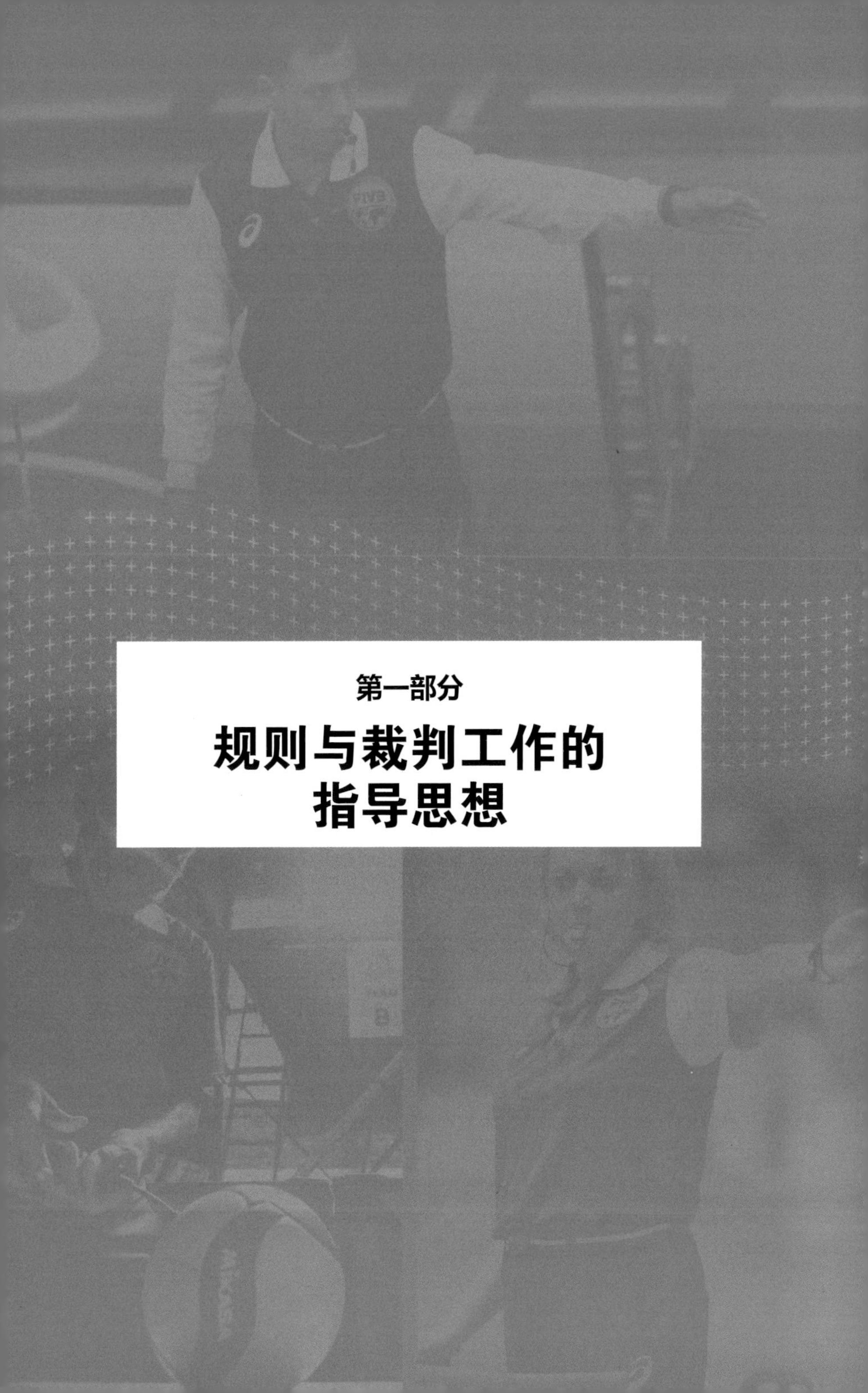

第一部分

规则与裁判工作的指导思想

INTRODUCTION

By every measure, Volleyball is one of the world' s top sports – it has more affiliated federations, larger TV viewing figures, larger followers at social media, greater numbers of registered and recreational players, than almost any other sport, and an image which is dynamic, clean and colorful, combining highly competitive sport and high-level show.

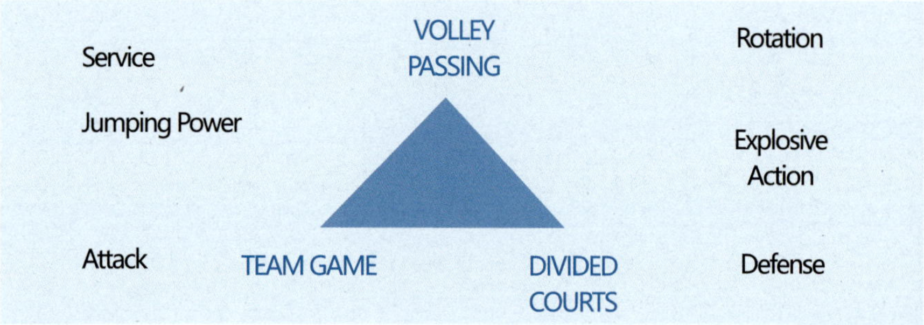

William Morgan, the game' s creator, would still recognize it because Volleyball has retained certain distinctive and essential elements over the years. Some of these it shares with other net/ball/ racquet games: – Service – Rotation (taking turns to serve) – Attack – Defense – players able to play at the net and in the back of the court. But the sport has moved on. It is explosive, it is spectacular, it is fast and free flowing, it has athletic players doing sensational things on court in crowed venues.

Additionally, Volleyball is unique amongst net games in insisting that the ball is in constant flight – a flying ball – and by allowing each team a degree of internal passing before the ball must be returned to the opponents, creating a kind sharing of the ball to produce equal opportunities for scoring points.

In recent years the FIVB has made great strides in adapting the game to a modern audience, liberalising the criteria for ball handling, introducing up to two specialist defensive "Libero" players, introducing the technology with the Video Challenge System providing fairness to the effort of the athletes and encouraging policies which promote flowing play to entertain the public, both at venue and on the screen.

前言

无论从哪个维度看，排球都是世界顶级运动之一。与其他大部分运动相比，排球拥有更多的会员协会，更高的电视收视率，更多的社交媒体粉丝，更多的注册运动员和业余爱好者。排球具有充满活力、纯净多彩的形象，集高水平的竞技性与精彩的表演性于一体。

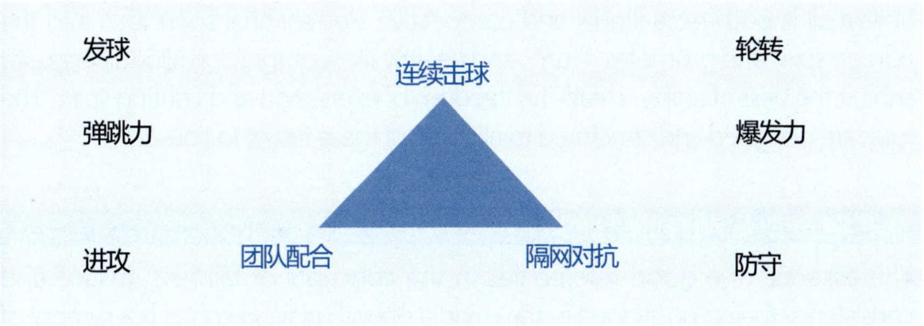

排球运动多年来一直保留着其独特的基本元素，相信它的创造者威廉·摩根时至今日仍会认出这项运动。排球与其他隔网对抗类项目有一些相似之处：→发球→轮转（轮换发球）→进攻→防守→运动员既可以在网前也可以在后排场区参与比赛。当然，这项运动也在不断进化。它爆发力十足、精彩纷呈，快速而流畅，排球运动员们在观众云集的场馆里奉献上激动人心的比赛。

此外，与其他隔网对抗类项目相比，排球的独特性在于追求让球持续在空中飞翔不落地。“让球飞起来”，给予每支球队一定次数的触球机会后必须把球交与对方，通过分享球权使双方获得平等的得分机会。

近年来，国际排联（FIVB）为适应现代球迷的观赏需求推动排球运动跨越式发展，包括放开控球标准、引入“双自由防守队员”、引入“视频挑战系统”技术为运动员提供公平的竞赛条件、鼓励实施能够提升比赛流畅性让现场和电视观众享乐比赛的政策措施。

THE RULES TEXT

This text is aimed at a broad Volleyball public – players, coaches, referees, spectators, commentators, and others – because an understanding of the rules allows better play and personal satisfaction – coaches can create better team structure and tactics, giving players full rein to display their skills, and an understanding of the relationship between written rules and actual actions on the court allows officials to make better decisions.

Volleyball is both recreational and competitive. Recreational sport taps into the human spirit and promotes "fun" and healthy life. Competition allows people to exhibit the best of ability, creativity, freedom of expression and fighting spirit. The rules are designed and structured to allow all of these facets to flourish.

THE REFEREE WITHIN THIS FRAMEWORK

The essence of a good referee lies in the concepts of fairness, justice and consistency (being positioned in the middle of both playing courts is a symbol of balance). Together these allow the players to trust the referee's actions. However, the referee must be a facilitator rather than a controller, an orchestra director rather than a dictator, an efficient promoter rather than an "efficient" punisher.

By understanding the reason why a rule has been written and by being clear about its purpose within the framework of the "show", the referee becomes a big part of the overall successful production, while remaining largely in the background and intervening only when necessary. We can say that a good referee will use the rules to make the competition a fulfilling experience for all concerned.

To those who have read thus far, view the rules which follow as the current state of development of a great game, but keep in mind why these preceding few paragraphs may be of equal importance to you in your own position within the sport.

Get involved !

Keep the ball flying !

Understand the game !

规则文本

本规则面向广大的排球运动参与者，包括运动员、教练员、裁判员、观众、解说人员等，因为只有正确理解规则才能更好地投入比赛和提升个人满意度。教练员能够更好地设计阵容和战术，充分发挥运动员能力；裁判员和技术官员能够更好地对照书面规则理解赛场实际情况从而做出更正确的决定。

排球运动兼具娱乐性和竞技性。其娱乐性体现了人文精神，促进“乐趣”和健康的生活方式。其竞技性让人们展现最好的竞技能力、创造力、自由表达力和拼搏精神。规则的设计和架构正是为促使所有这些要素蓬勃发展。

本规则框架内的裁判员

一名优秀裁判员的本质在于公平、公正和一致性（裁判位置设在双方比赛场区的中间即是平衡的象征）。这些本质特征使运动员能够信任裁判员的判罚。然而，裁判员必须是辅助者而不是控制者，是乐团指挥家而不是独裁者，是有效的推动者而不是“高效”的惩罚者。

通过理解一条规则制定的原因，明确这条规则在“表演”组织体系中的意图，裁判员就会成为比赛整体成功的重要一环，尽管他大部分时间身处幕后，只在必要时进行干预。可以说，一名优秀的裁判员能够运用规则让比赛成为令所有参与者满意的体验。

所有阅读至此的朋友们，下述规则体现了排球这项伟大运动的发展现状，请在详读规则的同时思考这篇前言对参与这项运动的你来讲是否同等重要。

积极参与！

让排球飞翔！

领悟比赛！

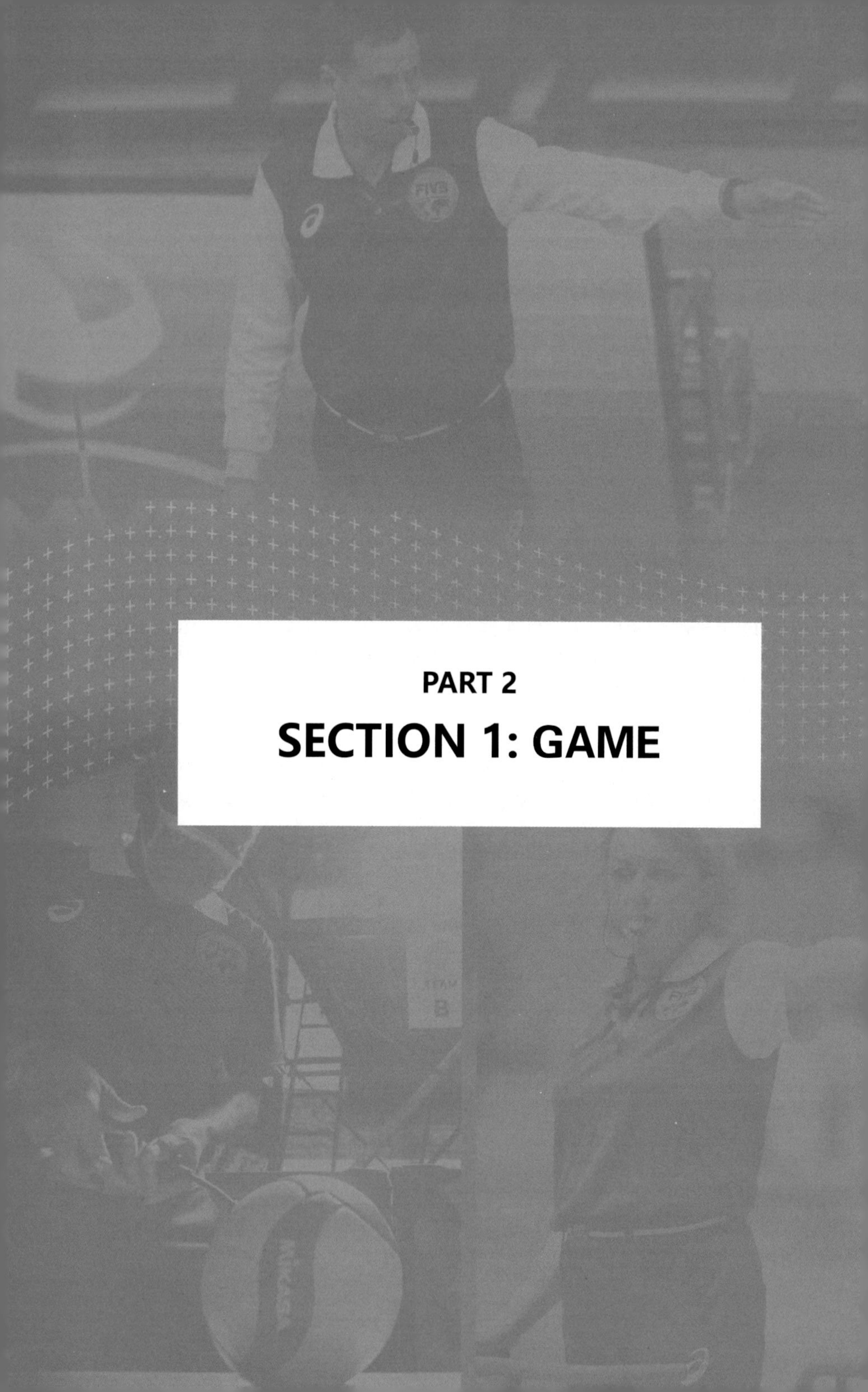

PART 2

SECTION 1: GAME

第二部分

第一章：比赛

CHAPTER 1
FACILITIES AND EQUIPMENT

See Rules

1 PLAYING AREA

The playing area includes the playing court and the free zone. It shall be rectangular and symmetrical. 1.1, D1a, D1b

1.1 DIMENSIONS

D2

The playing court is a rectangle measuring 18 m x 9 m, surrounded by a free zone which is a minimum of 3 m wide on all sides.

The free playing space is the space above the playing area which is free from any obstructions. The free playing space shall measure a minimum of 7 m in height from the playing surface.

For FIVB, World and Official Competitions, the free zone shall measure of 5 m from the side lines and 6.5 m from the end lines. The free playing space shall measure a minimum of 12.5 m in height from the playing surface.

1.2 PLAYING SURFACE

1.2.1 The surface must be flat, horizontal and uniform. It must not present any danger of injury to the players. It is forbidden to play on rough or slippery surfaces.

第一节
器材与设备

参照规则

1　比赛场地

比赛场地为对称的长方形，包括比赛场区和无障碍区。

1.1，图 1a，图 1b

1.1　面积

比赛场区为 18 米×9 米的长方形，其四周至少有 3 米宽的无障碍区。

图 2

比赛场区上空的无障碍空间从地面量起至少高 7 米，其间不得有任何障碍物。

国际排联（FIVB）比赛、世界性比赛和正式比赛中，比赛场区边线外的无障碍区的宽度应为 5 米，端线外的无障碍区的宽度应为 6.5 米。比赛场地上空的无障碍空间至少高 12.5 米。

1.2　比赛场地地面

1.2.1　场地的地面必须平坦、水平、划一，并不得有任何可能伤害队员的隐患。不得在湿滑或粗糙的地面上比赛。

For FIVB, World and Official Competitions, only a wooden or synthetic surface is allowed. Any surface must be previously approved by the FIVB.

1.2.2 On indoor courts the surface of the playing court must be of a light colour.

For FIVB, World and Official Competitions, white colours are required for the lines. Other colours, different from each other, are required for the playing court and the free zone. The playing court may be of different colours differentiating the front zone and the back zone. 1.1, 1.3

1.2.3 On outdoor courts a slope of 5 mm per metre is allowed for drainage. Court lines made of solid materials are forbidden. 1.3

1.3 LINES ON THE COURT D2

1.3.1 All lines are 5 cm wide. They must be of a light colour which is different from the colour of the floor and from any other lines. 1.2.2

1.3.2 Boundary lines

Two side lines and two end lines mark the playing court. Both side lines and end lines are drawn inside the dimensions of the playing court. 1.1

1.3.3 Centre line

The axis of the centre line divides the playing court into two equal courts measuring 9 m x 9 m each; however the entire width of the line is considered to belong to both courts equally. This line extends beneath the net from side line to side line. D2

国际排联（FIVB）比赛、世界性比赛和正式比赛中的场地地面只能是木制或合成物质的。任何地面都必须事先经国际排联（FIVB）验准。

1.2.2　室内比赛场区的地面必须为浅色。

国际排联（FIVB）比赛、世界性比赛和正式比赛中的场地界线为白色。比赛场区和无障碍区分别为另外的、彼此不同的颜色。比赛场区的前场区和后场区可使用不同颜色进行区分。 1.1，1.3

1.2.3　室外场地为了排水，每米可以有 5 毫米的坡度。禁止用任何坚硬的物体作为场地界线。 1.3

1.3　场地上的画线

图 2

1.3.1　所有的线宽 5 厘米。其颜色应该是与地面以及其他画线不同的浅色。 1.2.2

1.3.2　界线

两条边线和两条端线划定了比赛场区。边线和端线都包括在比赛场区的面积之内。 1.1

1.3.3　中线

中线在球网下方连接两条边线的中点。中线的宽度须平均分配，其中心线将比赛场区分为长 9 米、宽 9 米的两个相等场区。 图 2

1.3.4 Attack line

On each court, an attack line, whose rear edge is drawn 3 m back from the axis of the centre line, marks the front zone. 1.3.3, 1.4.1

For FIVB, World and Official Competitions, the attack line is extended by the addition of broken lines from the side lines, with five 15 cm short lines 5 cm wide, drawn 20 cm from each other to a total length of 1.75 m. D2

1.4 ZONES AND AREAS D1b, D2

1.4.1 Front zone 19.3.1.4, 23.3.2.3e, D2

On each court the front zone is limited by the axis of the centre line and the rear edge of the attack line. 1.3.3, 1.3.4, 19.3.1.4, 23.3.2.3e

The front zone is considered to extend beyond the side lines to the end of the free zone. 1.1, 1.3.2

1.4.2 Service zone

The service zone is a 9 m wide area behind each end line.

It is laterally limited by two short lines, each 15 cm long, drawn 20 cm behind the end line as an extension of the side lines. Both short lines are included in the width of the service zone. 1.3.2,12, D1b

In depth, the service zone extends to the end of the free zone. 1.1

1.4.3 Substitution zone

The substitution zone is limited by the extension of both attack lines up to the scorer's table. 1.3.4, 15.10.1, D1b

1.3.4 进攻线

每个场区各画一条距离中线中心线 3 米的进攻线，标出前场区。 1.3.3，1.4.1

国际排联（FIVB）比赛、世界性比赛和正式比赛时，进攻线是被无限延长的，在每条进攻线两端向无障碍区各画 5 段长 15 厘米、宽 5 厘米、间隔 20 厘米的虚线，虚线总长 1.75 米。 图 2

1.4 区与区域

图 1b，图 2

1.4.1 前场区

19.3.1.4，23.3.2.3e，图 2

每片场区里，中线中心线与进攻线之间的区域为前场区。 1.3.3，1.3.4，19.3.1.4，23.3.2.3e

前场区被认为是向边线外延长的，直至无障碍区的边界。 1.1，1.3.2

1.4.2 发球区

发球区宽 9 米，位置在端线后。

端线后两条边线的延长线各画一条长 15 厘米、垂直于端线并距离端线 20 厘米的短线。两条短线之间的区域为发球区，短线的宽度包括在发球区之内。 1.3.2，12，图 1b

发球区的深度延至无障碍区的终端。 1.1

1.4.3 换人区

两条进攻线的延长线之间、记录台一侧边线外的范围为换人区。 1.3.4，15.10.1，图 1b

1.4.4 Libero Replacement zone

The Libero Replacement zone is part of the free zone on the side of the team benches, limited by the extension of the attack line up to the end line. 19.3.2.7, D1b

1.4.5 Warm-up area

For FIVB, World and Official Competitions, the warm-up areas, sized approximately 3 m x 3 m, are located in both of the benchside corners, outside the free zone, where they will not obstruct the view of spectators, or alternatively behind the team bench, where the tribune starts above 2.5 m from the court surface. 24.2.5, D1a, D1b,

1.5 TEMPERATURE

The minimum temperature shall not be below 10° C (50° F).

For FIVB, World and Official Competitions, the maximum temperature shall be determined by the FIVB Technical Delegate of the match.

1.6 LIGHTING

Lighting should be no less than 300 lux. 1

For FIVB, World and Official Competitions, the lighting on the playing area should be not less than 2000 lux measured at 1 m above the surface of the playing area.

2 NET AND POSTS D3

2.1 HEIGHT OF THE NET

2.1.1 Placed vertically over the centre line there is a net whose top is set at the height of 2.43 m for men and 2.24 m for women. 1.3.3, 2.1.2

1.4.4　自由防守队员替换区

自由防守队员替换区是无障碍区的一部分，在替补席一侧的进攻线延长线和端线延长线之间。 19.3.2.7, 图 1b

1.4.5　准备活动区

国际排联（FIVB）比赛、世界性比赛和正式比赛中，位于双方无障碍区外的球队席远端角落应各画有 3 米 × 3 米的准备活动区，但不可阻挡观众的视线；如果观众看台的高度高于场地表面 2.5 米以上时，也可把准备活动区设置在球队席后面。 24.2.5, 图 1a, 图 1b

1.5　温度

最低温度不得低于 10°C (50°F)。

国际排联（FIVB）比赛、世界性比赛和正式比赛的室内最高温度由该场比赛的技术代表决定。

1.6　照明

光照强度应不低于 300 勒克斯。 1

国际排联（FIVB）比赛、世界性比赛和正式比赛中，场地的光照强度在距离场地地面 1 米处进行测量，数值应不得低于 2000 勒克斯。

2　球网与网柱

图 3

2.1　球网高度

2.1.1　球网架设在中线上空，高度为男子 2.43 米，女子 2.24 米。 1.3.3, 2.1.2

2.1.2 Its height is measured from the centre of the playing court. The net height (over the two side lines) must be exactly the same and must not exceed the official height by more than 2 cm. 1.1, 1.3.2, 2.1.1

2.2 STRUCTURE

The net is 1 m wide (± 3 cm) and 9.50 to 10 m long (with 25 to 50 cm on each side of the side bands), made of 10 cm square black mesh. D3

For FIVB, World and Official Competitions, in conjunction with specific competition regulations, the mesh may be modified to facilitate advertising according to marketing agreements.

At its top a horizontal band, 7 cm wide, made of two-fold white canvas, is sewn along its full length. Each extreme end of the band has a hole, through which passes a cord, fastening the band to the posts for keeping its top taut.

Within the band, a flexible cable fastens the net to the posts and keeps its top taut.

At the bottom of the net there is another horizontal band, 5 cm wide, similar to the top band, through which is threaded a rope. This rope fastens the net to the posts and keeps its lower part taut.

2.3 SIDE BANDS

Two white bands are fastened vertically to the net and placed directly above each side line. 1.3.2, D3

They are 5 cm wide and 1 m long and are considered as part of the net.

2.1.2　球网的高度应从场地中间丈量，球网两端（边线上空）的高度必须相等，并不得超过规定网高 2 厘米。 1.1, 1.3.2, 2.1.1

2.2 构造

球网宽 1 米（ ± 3 厘米），长 9.50~10 米（含每侧标志带外 25~50 厘米的部分），由 10 厘米见方的黑色网格编织而成。 图 3

国际排联（FIVB）比赛、世界性比赛和正式比赛中，可根据赛事商业开发协议调整网格大小以适应广告放置的需求，其变化应在竞赛规程中说明。

球网上沿的全长缝有一条 7 厘米宽的双层白帆布带。帆布带的两端各留有一个孔，用绳索穿过孔系在网柱上使球网上沿被拉紧。

在帆布带内，一根柔韧的绳索将球网固定在网柱上并使其顶部绷紧。

沿球网下沿的全长缝有另外一条构造与球网上沿相同的 5 厘米宽的帆布带，同样用一根绳索穿过它，系在网柱上使球网下沿绷紧。

2.3 标志带

两条宽 5 厘米、长 1 米的白色带子为标志带，分别系在球网的两端，垂直于边线。标志带被认为是球网的一部分。 1.3.2, 图 3

2.4 ANTENNAE

An antenna is a flexible rod, 1.80 m long and 10 mm in diameter, made of fiberglass or similar material.

An antenna is fastened at the outer edge of each side band. The antennae are placed on opposite sides of the net. 2.3, D3

The top 80 cm of each antenna extends above the net and is marked with 10 cm stripes of contrasting colour, preferably red and white.

The antennae are considered as part of the net and laterally delimit the crossing space. 10.1.1, D3, D5a, D5b

2.5 POSTS

2.5.1 The posts supporting the net are placed at a distance of 0.50-1.00 m outside the side lines. They are 2.55 m high and preferably adjustable. D3

For all FIVB, World and Official Competitions, the posts supporting the net are placed at a distance of 1 m outside the side lines and must be padded.

2.5.2 The posts are rounded and smooth, fixed to the ground without wires. There shall be no dangerous or obstructing devices.

2.6 ADDITIONAL EQUIPMENT

All additional equipment is determined by FIVB regulations.

2.4 标志杆

标志杆是有韧性的杆子，长 1.8 米，直径 10 毫米，由玻璃纤维或类似的材料制成。

两根标志杆分别设置在标志带外沿球网的不同侧面。 2.3, 图 3

每根标志杆高出球网 80 厘米，高出部分每 10 厘米应涂有明显对比的颜色，最好为红白相间。

标志杆被认为是球网的一部分，并视为过网区的边界。 10.1.1, 图 3, D5a, D5b

2.5 网柱

2.5.1 两根网柱分别架设在两条边线外 0.5~1 米处，高 2.55 米，最好可以调节高度。 图 3

国际排联（FIVB）比赛、世界性比赛和正式比赛中，网柱应架设在边线外 1 米处，其外部必须进行柔软包裹。

2.5.2 网柱应为光滑的圆形且无拉链。一切危险设施和障碍物都必须清除。

2.6 附加设备

一切附加设备都必须符合国际排联（FIVB）的规定。

3 BALLS

3.1 STANDARDS

The ball shall be spherical, made of a flexible leather or synthetic leather case with a bladder inside, made of rubber or a similar material.

Its colour may be a uniform light colour or a combination of colours.

Synthetic leather material and colour combinations of balls used in international official competitions should comply with FIVB standards.

Its circumference is 65-67 cm and its weight is 260-280 g.

Its inside pressure shall be 0.30 to 0.325 kg/cm2 (4.26 to 4.61 psi) (294.3 to 318.82 mbar or hPa).

3.2 UNIFORMITY OF BALLS

All balls used in a match must have the same standards regarding circumference, weight, pressure, type, colour, etc. 3.1

FIVB, World and Official Competitions, as well as National or League Championships, must be played with FIVB approved balls, unless by agreement of FIVB.

3.3 BALL RETRIEVAL SYSTEM

For FIVB, World and Official Competitions, five balls shall be used. In this case, six ball retrievers are stationed, one at each corner of the free zone and one behind each referee. D10

3　球

3.1　标准

球是圆形的，由柔软皮革或合成革制成外壳，内装橡胶或类似材料制成的球胆。

颜色可以是一色的浅色或彩色。

正式国际比赛使用的合成革和彩色球必须符合国际排联（FIVB）标准。

球的周长为 65~67 厘米，重量为 260~280 克。

球的气压应为 0.30~0.325 千克 / 平方厘米（4.26~4.61 磅力 / 平方英寸）(294.3~ 318.82 百帕）。

3.2　统一性

在同一次比赛中所用的球，其周长、重量、气压、牌号及颜色等都必须是统一标准的。 3.1

除非国际排联（FIVB）同意，否则，国际排联（FIVB）比赛、世界性比赛和正式比赛与国家锦标赛、国家联赛一样，都必须使用国际排联（FIVB）批准的用球。

3.3　5 球制

国际排联（FIVB）比赛、世界性比赛和正式比赛采用 5 球制。这种情况下，应设 6 名捡球员：无障碍区的 4 个角落各 1 名，第 1、2 裁判员身后各 1 名。 图 10

CHAPTER 2
PARTICIPANTS

See Rules

4 TEAMS

4.1 TEAM COMPOSITION

4.1.1 For the match, a team may consist of up to 12 players, plus 5.2, 5.3

- Coaching Staff: one coach, **a maximum of two assistant coaches,**
- Medical Staff: one **team therapist** and one medical doctor.

Only those listed on the score sheet may normally enter the Competition/Control Area and take part in the official warm up and in the match.

For FIVB, World and Official competitions for Seniors:

Up to 14 players may be recorded on the score sheet and play in a match.

The maximum five staff members on the bench (including the coach) are chosen by the coach him/herself but must be listed on the score sheet, and be registered on the O-2(bis).

The team Manager and/or team Journalist may not sit on or behind the bench in the Control Area.

第二节
比赛参加者

参照规则

4 比赛队

4.1 队的组成

4.1.1 一场比赛中，一支球队可以由最多 12 名队员及以下人员组成： 5.2, 5.3

- 教练成员：一名教练员、**最多两名助理教练员**；

- 医疗成员：一名**理疗师**和一名医生。

只有登记在记录表上队的成员才可以进入比赛 / 控制区，参加赛前的正式准备活动和比赛。

国际排联（FIVB）比赛、世界性比赛和正式比赛中的成年比赛：

最多可有 14 名队员被登记在记录表上并参加比赛。

经教练员指定，最多 5 名官员（包括教练员）可以坐在球队席上，这 5 人必须登记在记录表和 O-2（bis）表上。

领队或随队记者不可以坐在球队席或球队席后面的控制区。

Any Medical doctor or team therapist used in FIVB, World and Official Competitions must be part of the official Delegation and accredited beforehand by the FIVB. However, for FIVB, World and Official Competitions for Seniors, if they are not included as members on the team bench, they must sit against the delimitation fence, inside the Competition–Control Area or sit in a special place indicated in the Specific Competition Handbook and may only intervene if invited by the referees to deal with an emergency to the players. The team therapist (even if not on the bench) may assist with the warm up until the start of the official net warm up session. D1a 7.2.1

The Official Regulations for each event will be found in the Specific Competition Handbook.

4.1.2 One of the players is the team captain, who shall be indicated on the score sheet. 5.1

4.1.3 Only the players recorded on the score sheet may enter the court and play in the match. Once the coach and the team captain have signed the score sheet, (team list for electronic score sheet) the recorded players cannot be changed. 1, 4.1.1, 5.1.1, 5.2.2

4.2 LOCATION OF THE TEAM

4.2.1 The players not in play should either sit on their team bench or be in their warm-up area. The coach and other team members sit on the bench, but may temporarily leave it. 1.4.5, 5.2.3, 7.3.3

The benches for the teams are located beside the scorer's table, outside the free zone. D1a, D1b

4.2.2 Only the team composition members are permitted to enter the playing area, to sit on the bench during the match and to participate in the official warm-up session. 4.1.1, 7.2

国际排联（FIVB）比赛、世界性比赛和正式比赛中，医生或理疗师必须是球队的成员，而且须在赛前通过国际排联认证。但是，国际排联（FIVB）比赛、世界性比赛和正式比赛中的成年比赛，如果医生或理疗师不属于坐在球队席的 5 名官员时，则必须坐在比赛控制区内的隔离板附近，或者坐在技术手册规定的专门位置。在裁判员示意允许其处理场上队员的突发伤病时才能进入场地。理疗师（即使未坐在球队席）可以协助球队进行热身活动，直至正式准备活动开始。 图 1a

7.2.1

每项赛事的竞赛规程须体现在各自比赛的技术手册中。

4.1.2 球队中任何 1 名队员可担任队长，并注明在记录表上。 5.1

4.1.3 只有登记在记录表上的队员才可以进入场地和参加比赛。教练员和队长在记录表上签字以后，已登记在记录表（或电子记录表）上的队员名单不得更改。 1, 4.1.1, 5.1.1 5.2.2

4.2 队的位置

4.2.1 比赛时，替补队员应坐在本队的球队席或在本队的准备活动区内。教练员和球队其他成员也应坐在球队席上，但可暂时离开。 1.4.5, 5.2.3, 7.3.3

球队席设在记录台的两侧、无障碍区之外。 图 1a, 图 1b

4.2.2 只有球队的成员才被允许进入比赛场地，在比赛期间坐在球队席，并参加正式的赛前准备活动。 4.1.1, 7.2

4.2.3 Players not in play may warm-up without balls as follows:

4.2.3.1 during play: in the warm-up areas; 1.4.5, D1a, D1b

4.2.3.2 during time-outs: in the free zone behind their court. 1.3.3, 15.4

4.2.4 During set intervals, players may warm-up using balls within their own free zone. 18.1

4.3 EQUIPMENT

A player's equipment consists of a jersey, shorts, socks (the uniform) and sport shoes.

4.3.1 The colour and the design for the jerseys, shorts and socks must be uniform for the team (except for the Libero). The uniforms must be clean. 4.1, 19.2

4.3.2 The shoes must be light and pliable with rubber or composite soles without heels.

4.3.3 Players' jerseys must be numbered from 1 to 20. 4.3.3.2

In FIVB, World and Official Competitions for Seniors, where larger playing squads are used, numbers may be extended.

4.3.3.1 The number must be placed on the jersey at the centre of the front and of the back. The colour and brightness of the numbers must contrast with the colour and brightness of the jerseys.

4.3.3.2 The number must be a minimum of 15 cm in height on the chest, and a minimum of 20 cm in height on the back. The stripe forming the numbers shall be a minimum of 2 cm in width.

4.3.4 The team captain must have on his/her jersey a stripe of 8 cm x 2 cm underlining the number on the chest. 5.1

4.2.3　替补队员可以做无球的准备活动，具体如下：

4.2.3.1　比赛中：在准备活动区内； 1.4.5, 图 1a, 图 1b

4.2.3.2　暂停时：在本方场区之后的无障碍区内。 1.3.3, 15.4

4.2.4　两局比赛之间，队员可以在各自球队的无障碍区内使用球做准备活动。 18.1

4.3　装备

队员的装备包括上衣、短裤、袜子(比赛服)和运动鞋。

4.3.1　全队上衣、短裤和袜子的颜色及式样必须统一(*自由防守队员除外*)，比赛服必须整洁。 4.1, 19.2

4.3.2　运动鞋必须柔软、轻便，鞋底应为没有后跟的胶底或合成革。

4.3.3　队员上衣必须有号码，序号为 1~20。 4.3.3.2

国际排联(FIVB)比赛、世界性比赛和正式比赛中的成年比赛，如遇赛期较长、赛程分散且允许报名人数较多的情况，队员号码可以向 20 之后顺延。

4.3.3.1　号码必须在身前和身后的中间位置，并与上衣的颜色明显不同。

4.3.3.2　胸前号码至少高 15 厘米，背后号码至少高 20 厘米，号码笔画至少宽 2 厘米。

4.3.4　队长上衣胸前号码下应有一条长 8 厘米、宽 2 厘米的带状标志。 5.1

4.3.5 It is forbidden to wear uniforms of a colour different from that of the other players (except for the Liberos), and/or without official numbers. 19.2

4.4 CHANGE OF EQUIPMENT

The 1st referee may authorize one or more players: 23

4.4.1 to play barefoot;

4.4.2 to change wet or damaged uniforms between sets or after substitution, provided that the colour, design and number of the new uniform(s) are the same; 4.3, 15.5

4.4.3 to play in training suits in cold weather, provided that they are of the same colour and design for the whole team (except for the Liberos) and numbered according to Rule 4.3.3. 4.1.1, 19.2

4.5 FORBIDDEN OBJECTS

4.5.1 It is forbidden to wear objects which may cause injury or give an artificial advantage to the player.

4.5.2 Players may wear glasses or lenses at their own risk.

4.5.3 Compression pads (padded injury protection devices) may be worn for protection or support.

For FIVB, World and Official competitions for Seniors, these devices must be of the same colour as the corresponding part of the uniform. Black, white or neutral colours may be also used provided that all using players wear the same colour.

5 TEAM LEADERS

Both the team captain and the coach are responsible for the conduct and discipline of their team members. 20

4.3.5　禁止穿着不符合规则规定号码的服装或与同队其他队员不同颜色的服装（*自由防守队员除外*）。　19.2

4.4　服装的更换

第 1 裁判员可以允许 1 名或多名队员：　23

4.4.1　赤脚比赛；

4.4.2　局间或换人后更换浸湿或损坏的服装，但必须是相同的颜色、式样和号码；　4.3, 15.5

4.4.3　天气较冷穿训练服比赛时，全队服装颜色、式样必须相同（*自由防守队员除外*），号码符合规则 4.3.3 规定。　4.1.1, 19.2

4.5　禁止佩戴的物品

4.5.1　禁止佩戴可能对队员造成伤害或增加助力的物品。

4.5.2　队员可以戴眼镜或隐形眼镜比赛，但风险自负。

4.5.3　可以使用加压护具（带护垫的损伤防护器具）进行保护或支撑。

国际排联（FIVB）比赛、世界性比赛和正式比赛中的成年比赛，此类护具的颜色必须与比赛服的某一部分一致。黑色、白色或中性颜色也被允许使用，前提是所有使用者穿戴的颜色相同。

5　队的领导

队长和教练员都应对全队成员的行为和纪律负责。　20

The Liberos can be either team or game captain.

5.1 CAPTAIN

5.1.1 PRIOR TO THE MATCH, the team captain represents his/her team in the toss, then signs the score sheet. 7.1, 25.2.1.1

5.1.2 DURING THE MATCH and while on the court, the team captain is the game captain. When the team captain is not on the court, the coach or the team captain must assign another player on the court, to assume the role of game captain. This game captain maintains his/her responsibilities until he/she is substituted, or the team captain returns to play, or the set ends. 15.2.1

When the ball is out of play, only the game captain is authorized to speak to the referees: 8.2

5.1.2.1 to ask for an explanation on the application or interpretation of the Rules, and also to submit the requests or questions of his/her teammates. If the game captain does not agree with the explanation of the 1st referee, he/she may choose to protest against such decision and immediately indicates to the 1st referee that he/she reserves the right to record an official protest on the score sheet at the end of the match; 23.2.4

5.1.2.2 to ask authorization:

a) to change all or part of the equipment, 4.3, 4.4.2
b) to verify the positions of the teams, 7.4, 7.6
c) to check the floor, the net, the ball, etc.; 1.2, 2, 3

5.1.2.3 in the absence of the coach unless the team has an assistant coach who has overtaken the coach's functions to request time-outs and substitutions. 5.2, 5.3, 15.3.1, 15.4.1, 15.5.2

自由防守队员可以担任队长和场上队长。

5.1 队长

5.1.1 比赛前， 队长在记录表上签字 ，并代表本队抽签。 7.1, 25.2.1.1

5.1.2 比赛中，当队长在场上时，他就是场上队长。当队长不在场上时，教练员或队长必须指定另一名场上队员担任场上队长并代行其职责，直至该队员被替换下场，或队长返回场上，或至该局比赛结束。 15.2.1

当比赛成死球时，只有场上队长有权与裁判员讲话： 8.2

5.1.2.1 请求对规则和规则的执行进行解释、转达本队成员提出的请求或问题。如果他对解释不满意，可以选择抗议并立即向第 1 裁判员声明保留其在比赛结束时将正式抗议写在记录表上的权利。 23.2.4

5.1.2.2 请求允许：

a) 更换全部或部分设备； 4.3, 4.4.2
b) 核对双方队员的位置； 7.4, 7.6
c) 检查地板、球网和球等。 1.2, 2, 3

5.1.2.3 在教练员缺席且没有助理教练员代行其职责时，请求暂停和换人。 5.2, 5.3, 15.3.1, 15.4.1, 15.5.2

5.1.3	AT THE END OF THE MATCH, the team captain:	6.3
5.1.3.1	thanks the referees and signs the score sheet to ratify the result;	25.2.3.3
5.1.3.2	may, when it has been notified in due time to the 1st referee, confirm and record on the score sheet an official protest regarding the referee' s application or interpretation of the rules.	5.1.2.1, 25.2.3.2

5.2 COACH

5.2.1	Throughout the match, the coach conducts the play of his/her team from outside the playing court. He/she selects the starting line-ups, the substitutes, and takes time-outs. In these functions his/her contacting official is the 2nd referee.	1.1, 7.3.2, 15.4.1,15.5.2
5.2.2	PRIOR TO THE MATCH, the coach records or checks the names and numbers of his/her players on the score sheet team roster, and then signs it.	4.1, 19.1.3, 25.2.1.1
5.2.3	DURING THE MATCH, the coach:	
5.2.3.1	prior to each set, gives the 2nd referee or the scorer the line-up sheet(s) duly filled in and signed; If Tablet apps are used, the electronic transmission of the line-up is automatically deemed to be official.	7.3.2, 7.4, 7.6
5.2.3.2	sits on the team bench nearest to the scorer, but may leave it;	4.2
5.2.3.3	requests time-outs and substitutions;	15.4, 15.5
5.2.3.4	may, as well as other team members, give instructions to the players on the court. The coach may give these instructions while standing or walking within the	1.3.4, 1.4.5, D1a,D1b, D2

5.1.3 比赛结束时，队长： 6.3

5.1.3.1 感谢裁判员，并在记录表上签字承认比赛结果； 25.2.3.3

5.1.3.2 如果他曾向第1裁判员提出过声明，在经过进一步确认后可在记录表上记录关于对裁判员规则执行或解释的正式抗议。 5.1.2.1, 25.2.3.2

5.2 教练员

5.2.1 教练员应自始至终在比赛场区之外进行指挥。他与第2裁判员联系填写位置表、换人或请求暂停。 1.1, 7.3.2, 15.4.1,15.5.2

5.2.2 比赛前，教练员在记录表上登记和检查队员姓名、号码并签字。 4.1, 19.1.3, 25.2.1.1

5.2.3 比赛中，教练员：

5.2.3.1 每局开始前填写位置表，签字后交给第2裁判员或记录员。如果是使用电子设备的比赛，则该位置表的电子传送过程将自动被视为正式提交。 7.3.2, 7.4, 7.6

5.2.3.2 坐在最靠近记录员一端的球队席上，但可以暂时离开。 4.2

5.2.3.3 请求暂停或换人。 15.4, 15.5

5.2.3.4 与球队的其他成员一样，都可以在场上对队员进行指导。教练员进行指导时，如果准备活动区位于比赛控制区的角落，教练员可以在本方球队席前自进 1.3.4, 1.4.5, 图1a, 图1b, 图2

free zone in front of his/her team's bench from the extension of the attack line up to the warm-up area, if situated in the corner of the Competition Control Area, without disturbing or delaying the match. Should the warm up area be situated behind the team bench, then the coach may move from the extension of the attack line up to the end of his/ her team's court, but without obstructing the view of the line judges.

5.3 ASSISTANT COACH

5.3.1 The assistant coach sits on the team bench, but has no right to intervene in the match. 4.2.1

5.3.2 Should the coach have to leave his/her team for any reason including sanction, but excluding entering the court as a player, an assistant coach may assume the coach's functions for the duration of the absence, once confirmed to the referee by the game captain. 5.1.2.3, 5.2

攻线延长线至准备活动区的无障碍区内站立或行走，但不得干扰或延误比赛。如果准备活动区位于球队席后面，教练员的活动范围可以自进攻线延至本方场地的边界，但不得阻挡司线员的视线。

5.3 助理教练员

5.3.1 助理教练员坐在球队席上，但无任何权力干预比赛。 4.2.1

5.3.2 如果教练员除作为队员上场外的任何原因（包括被处罚）必须离开球队时，1 名助理教练员可以在此期间承担教练员的职责，但必须经由场上队长向裁判员确认。 5.1.2.3, 5.2

CHAPTER 3
PLAYING FORMAT

See Rules

6 TO SCORE A POINT, TO WIN A SET AND THE MATCH

6.1 TO SCORE A POINT

6.1.1 Point

A team scores a point:

6.1.1.1 by successfully landing the ball on the opponent' s court; 8.3

6.1.1.2 when the opponent team commits a fault; 6.1.2

6.1.1.3 when the opponent team receives a penalty. 16.2.3, 21.3.1

6.1.2 Fault

A team commits a fault by making a playing action contrary to the rules (or by violating them in some other way). The referees judge the faults and determine the consequences according to the rules:

6.1.2.1 if two or more faults are committed successively, only the first one is counted;

6.1.2.2 if two or more faults are committed by opponents simultaneously, a DOUBLE FAULT is called and the rally is replayed. D11 (23)

第三节
比赛方法

参照规则

6　得 1 分、胜 1 局与胜 1 场

6.1　得 1 分

6.1.1　得分

以下情况球队得 1 分：

6.1.1.1　球成功落在对方场区；　8.3

6.1.1.2　对方犯规；　6.1.2

6.1.1.3　对方受到处罚。　16.2.3, 21.3.1

6.1.2　犯规

当队员的比赛行为违背规则（或其他方式的犯规）时，裁判员按以下规则做出判定：

6.1.2.1　如果 2 个或更多的犯规先后发生，只判第 1 个犯规；

6.1.2.2　如果双方队员同时犯规，判为“双方犯规”，该球重新进行。　图 11(23)

6.1.3 **Rally and completed rally**

A **rally** is the sequence of playing actions from the moment of the service hit by the server until the ball is out of play. A **completed rally** is the sequence of playing actions which results in the award of a point. 8.1, 8.2, 12.2.2.1, 15.2.3, 15.11.1.3, 19.3.2.1, 19.3.2.9

This includes:
– the award of a penalty 21.3.1
– loss of service for service hit made after the time-limit. 12.4.4

6.1.3.1 If the serving team wins a rally, it scores a point and continues to serve.

6.1.3.2 If the receiving team wins a rally, it scores a point and it must serve next.

6.2 TO WIN A SET D11 (9)

A set (except the deciding 5th set) is won by the team which first scores 25 points with a minimum lead of two points. In the case of a 24-24 tie, play is continued until a two-point lead is achieved (26-24; 27-25; etc.). 6.3.2

6.3 TO WIN THE MATCH D11 (9)

6.3.1 The match is won by the team that wins three sets. 6.2

6.3.2 In the case of a 2-2 tie, the deciding 5th set is played to 15 points with a minimum lead of 2 points. 7.1

6.4 DEFAULT AND INCOMPLETE TEAM

6.4.1 If a team refuses to play after being summoned to do so, it is declared in default and forfeits the match with the result 0-3 for the match and 0-25 for each set. 6.2, 6.3

6.1.3 比赛过程和完整比赛过程

比赛过程是指从发球击球起至该球成死球的比赛行为。**完整比赛过程**是造成了得分结果的比赛行为。 8.1, 8.2, 12.2.2.1, 15.2.3, 15.11.1.3, 19.3.2.1, 19.3.2.9

包括：

— 判罚得分； 21.3.1

— 因发球超时犯规而失去发球权。 12.4.4

6.1.3.1 如果发球队获胜，得 1 分并继续发球；

6.1.3.2 如果接发球队获胜，得 1 分并获得发球权。

6.2 胜 1 局

图 11 (9)

每局（决胜的第 5 局除外）先得 25 分同时至少超过对方 2 分的队胜 1 局。当比分为 24-24 时，比赛继续进行至一支球队领先 2 分 (26-24、27-25……) 为止。 6.3.2

6.3 胜 1 场

图 11 (9)

6.3.1 胜 3 局的球队胜 1 场。 6.2

6.3.2 如果 2-2 平局时，决胜的第 5 局先得 15 分并至少领先对方 2 分的球队获胜。 7.1

6.4 弃权与阵容不完整

6.4.1 如果一支球队被召唤后拒绝比赛，则宣布该队弃权。对方以每局 25-0 的比分和 3-0 的局分获胜。 6.2, 6.3

6.4.2 A team that, without justifiable reason, does not appear on the playing court on time is declared in default with the same result as in Rule 6.4.1.

6.4.3 A team that is declared INCOMPLETE for the set or for the match, loses the set or the match. The opponent team is given the points, or the points and the sets, needed to win the set or the match. The incomplete team keeps its points and sets. 6.2, 6.3, 7.3.1

7 STRUCTURE OF PLAY

7.1 THE TOSS

Before the match, the 1st referee carries out a toss to decide upon the first service and the sides of the court in the first set. 12.1.1

If a deciding set is to be played, a new toss will be carried out. 6.3.2

7.1.1 The toss is taken in the presence of the two team captains. 5.1

7.1.2 The winner of the toss chooses:

EITHER

7.1.2.1 the right to serve or to receive the service, 12.1.1

OR

7.1.2.2 the side of the court.

The loser takes the remaining choice.

6.4.2　一支球队无正当理由而未准时到达比赛场地，则宣布该队弃权，结果同规则 6.4.1。

6.4.3　一支球队被宣布 1 局或 1 场比赛阵容不完整时，则输掉该局或该场比赛，判给对方胜该局或该场比赛所必要的分数和局数。保留阵容不完整的球队所得的分数和局数。 6.2, 6.3, 7.3.1

7　比赛的组织

7.1　抽签

比赛开始前由第 1 裁判员主持抽签，决定第 1 局首先发球的球队和场区。 12.1.1

进行决胜局比赛前，应再次抽签。 6.3.2

7.1.1　抽签由双方队长参加。 5.1

7.1.2　抽签获胜方可以选择：

7.1.2.1　发球或接发球； 12.1.1

或

7.1.2.2　场区。

另一方接受余下选择。

7.2 OFFICIAL WARM-UP SESSION

7.2.1 Prior to the match, if the teams have previously had a playing court exclusively at their disposal, they are entitled to a 6-minute official warm-up period together at the net; if not, they may have 10 minutes.

For FIVB, World and Official competitions, teams will be entitled to a 10 minute warm up period together at the net.

7.2.2 If either captain requests separate (consecutive) official warm-ups at the net, the teams are allowed 3 minutes each or 5 minutes each. 7.2.1

7.2.3 In the case of consecutive official warm-ups, the team that has the first service takes the first turn at the net. 7.1.2.1, 7.2.2

For FIVB, World and Official Competitions, all players must wear playing uniform for the complete Protocol and warm up.

7.3 TEAM STARTING LINE-UP

7.3.1 There must always be six players per team in play. 6.4.3

The team's starting line-up indicates the rotational order of the players on the court. This order must be maintained throughout the set. 7.6

7.3.2 Before the start of each set, the coach has to present the starting line-up of his/her team on a line-up sheet or via the electronic device, if used. The sheet is submitted, duly filled in and signed, to the 2nd referee or the scorer – or electronically sent directly to the e-scorer. 5.2.3.1, 24.3.1, 25.2.1.2

7.3.3 The players who are not in the starting line-up of a set are the substitutes for that set (except the Liberos). 7.3.2, 15.5

7.2 准备活动

7.2.1 在比赛开始前，如另有场地专门供比赛球队进行活动，他们可以共同上网活动 6 分钟；如果没有，他们可以活动 10 分钟。

国际排联（FIVB）比赛、世界性比赛和正式比赛中，比赛球队应共同上网活动 10 分钟。

7.2.2 如果任何一方队长要求分开使用球网进行准备活动，两队可以各自分练 3 分钟或 5 分钟。 7.2.1

7.2.3 如果两队分开进行准备活动，首先发球的球队先使用球网。 7.1.2.1, 7.2.2

国际排联（FIVB）比赛、世界性比赛和正式比赛中，所有队员必须穿着比赛服参与赛前仪式和准备活动。

7.3 球队首发阵容

7.3.1 每支球队必须始终保持 6 名队员进行比赛。 6.4.3

球队的位置表指明队员在场上的轮转次序，直至该局比赛结束。 7.6

7.3.2 每局比赛开始前，教练员应将首发阵容填写在位置表上或通过电子设备（如使用）提交。在正确填写并签字后，教练员应将其提交给第 2 裁判员或记录员，或者通过电子设备直接提交给电子记录员。 5.2.3.1, 24.3.1, 25.2.1.2

7.3.3 未列入本局首发阵容的队员，为该局的替补队员（自由防守队员外）。 7.3.2, 15.5

7.3.4 Once the line-up sheet has been delivered to the 2nd referee or scorer, no change in the line-up may be authorized without a regular substitution. 15.2.2, 15.5, D11 (5)

7.3.5 Discrepancies between players' position on court and on the line-up sheet are dealt with as follows: 24.3.1

7.3.5.1 when such a discrepancy is discovered before the start of the set, players' positions must be rectified according to those on the line-up sheet – there will be no sanction; 7.3.2

7.3.5.2 when, before the start of the set, any player on court is found not to be registered on the line-up sheet of that set, this player must be changed to conform to the line-up sheet – there will be no sanction; 7.3.2

7.3.5.3 however, if the coach wishes to keep such non-recorded player(s) on the court, he/she has to request regular substitution(s), by use of the corresponding hand signal, which will then be recorded on the score sheet. 15.2.2, D11 (5)

If a discrepancy between players' positions and the line-up sheet is discovered later, the team at fault must revert to the correct positions. The opponent's points remain valid and in addition they receive a point and the next service. All points scored by the team at fault from the exact moment of the fault up to the discovery of the fault are cancelled.

7.3.5.4 Where a player is found to be on court but he/she is not registered on the team roster, the opponent's points remain valid, and in addition they gain a point and service. The team at fault will lose all points and/or sets (0 : 25, if necessary) gained from the moment the non- registered player entered the court, and will have to submit a revised line-up sheet and send a new registered player into the court, in the position of the non-registered player. 6.1.2, 7.3.2

7.3.4　位置表一经提交给第 2 裁判员或记录员，则除正常换人外，该阵容不得更改。　15.2.2, 15.5, 图 11 (5)

7.3.5　当场上队员的位置与位置表不符时：　24.3.1

7.3.5.1　一局开始前，如发现场上队员的位置与位置表不符，必须按位置表进行纠正，无其他判处。　7.3.2

7.3.5.2　一局开始前，场上有任何队员被发现未登记在位置表上，则必须更换该队员使其与位置表相符，无其他判处。　7.3.2

7.3.5.3　如果教练员希望保持未登记在位置表上的队员首发上场，他必须以相应的手势请求正常换人，并登记在记录表上。　15.2.2, 图 11 (5)

如果队员的场上位置与位置表不符的情况没有被及时发现，则发现时位置错误的一方必须恢复正确站位；对方在所得比分被保留的同时得 1 分并获发球权。位置错误的一方在位置错误期间所得的分数一律被取消。

7.3.5.4　比赛进行中，一名没有在记录表上登记的队员被发现时，对方在所得比分被保留的同时得 1 分并获发球权，该队将失去这名队员上场后的所有比分或局数 (0 : 25，如有必要)，同时必须提交一份修正后的位置表，再选 1 名新的注册队员进场代替非注册队员的位置。　6.1.2, 7.3.2

7.4 POSITIONS

D4

At the moment the ball is hit by the server, each team must be positioned within its own court in the rotational order (except the server). 7.6.1, 8.1, 12.4

7.4.1 The positions of the players are numbered as follows:

7.4.1.1 the three players along the net are front-row players and occupy positions 4 (front-left), 3 (front-centre) and 2 (front-right);

7.4.1.2 the other three are back-row players occupying positions 5 (back-left), 6 (back-centre) and 1 (back-right).

7.4.2 Relative positions between players:

7.4.2.1 each back-row player must be positioned further back from the centre line than the corresponding front-row player;

7.4.2.2 the front-row players and the back-row players, respectively, must be positioned laterally in the order indicated in Rule 7.4.1.

7.4.3 The positions of players are determined and controlled according to the positions of their feet contacting the ground (the last contact with the floor fixes the player's position), as follows: D4

7.4.3.1 each back-row player must be level with or have at least a part of one foot further from the centre line than the front foot of the corresponding front-row player; 1.3.3, 7.4.2.1, 7.4.3

7.4.3.2 each right (left) side player must be level with or have at least a part of one foot closer to the right (left) sideline than the foot further from the right (left) side line of the other players in that row. 1.3.2, 7.4.1.2, 7.4.2.2, 7.4.3

7.4 位置

图 4

发球队员击球时，双方队员(发球队员除外)必须在本场区内按轮转次序站位。

7.6.1, 8.1, 12.4

7.4.1 队员的场上位置如下：

7.4.1.1 靠近球网的3名队员是前排队员，其位置为4号位(左)、3号位(中)和2号位(右)

7.4.1.2 另外3名队员是后排队员，其位置为5号位(左)、6号位(中)和1号位(右)。

7.4.2 队员相互间的位置关系：

7.4.2.1 每一名后排队员的位置必须比其相应的前排队员距离中线更远；

7.4.2.2 前排队员和后排队员必须分别按照规则7.4.1规定的顺序左右站位。

7.4.3 队员的位置应根据其脚最后与地面接触的部位进行判定，具体如下：

图 4

7.4.3.1 每一名后排队员要与同列前排队员的前脚平齐，或者至少有1只脚的一部分距离中线更远；

1.3.3, 7.4.2.1, 7.4.3

7.4.3.2 每一名右(左)边队员要与同排其他队员距右(左)侧边线的距离相同，或者至少有1只脚的一部分距右(左)侧边线更近。

1.3.2, 7.4.1.2, 7.4.2.2, 7.4.3

7.4.4 After the service hit, the players may move around and occupy any position on their court and the free zone.

7.5 POSITIONAL FAULT — D4, D11 (13)

7.5.1 The team commits a positional fault, if any player is not in his/her correct position at the moment the ball is hit by the server. When a player is on court through illegal substitution, and play restarts, this is counted as a positional fault with the consequences of an illegal substitution. — 7.3, 7.4, 15.9

7.5.2 If the server commits a serving fault at the moment of the service hit, the server's fault is counted before a positional fault. — 12.4, 12.7.1

7.5.3 If the service becomes faulty after the service hit, it is the positional fault that will be counted. — 12.7.2

7.5.4 A positional fault leads to the following consequences:

7.5.4.1 the team is sanctioned with a point and service to the opponent; — 6.1.3

7.5.4.2 players' positions must be rectified. — 7.3, 7.4

7.6 ROTATION

7.6.1 The rotational order is determined by the team's starting line-up and controlled with the service order and players' positions throughout the set. — 7.3.1, 7.4.1, 12.2

7.6.2 When the receiving team has gained the right to serve, its players rotate one position clock-wise: the player in position 2 rotates to position 1 to serve, the player in position 1 rotates to position 6, etc. — 12.2.2.2

7.4.4 发球击球后，队员可以在本方场区和无障碍区的任何位置活动。

7.5 位置错误

图4, 图11 (13)

7.5.1 当发球队员击球时，如果队员不在其正确位置上则该队构成位置错误犯规。当一名队员经不合法换人程序进入场内且比赛重新开始时，这将被视为位置错误，并承担不合法换人程序导致的后果。 7.3, 7.4, 15.9

7.5.2 当发球队员击球时的犯规与对方位置错误的犯规同时发生时，发球队员的犯规被认为在先。 12.4, 12.7.1

7.5.3 如果发球队员击球后的犯规与对方位置错误的犯规同时发生，则对方的位置错误犯规在先。 12.7.2

7.5.4 位置错误按如下步骤处理：

7.5.4.1 该队被判失去 1 分，由对方发球； 6.1.3

7.5.4.2 队员的位置必须被纠正。 7.3, 7.4

7.6 轮转

7.6.1 一局比赛中，轮转次序、发球次序以及队员位置的确定，均以位置表为依据。 7.3.1, 7.4.1, 12.2

7.6.2 接发球队获得发球权后，该队队员必须按顺时针方向轮转 1 个位置：2 号位队员转至 1 号位发球，1 号位队员转至 6 号位，等等。 12.2.2.2

7.7 ROTATIONAL FAULT D11 (13)

7.7.1 A rotational fault is committed when the SERVICE is not made according to the rotational order. It leads to the following consequences in order: 7.6.1, 12

7.7.1.1 the scorer stops play by the buzzer; the opponent gains a point and next service; 6.1.3

If the rotational fault is determined only after the completion of the rally which started with a rotational fault, only a single point is awarded to the opponent, regardless of the result of the rally played.

7.7.1.2 the rotational order of the faulty team must be rectified; 7.6.1

7.7.2 Additionally, the scorer should determine the exact moment when the fault was committed, and all points scored subsequently by the team at fault must be cancelled. The opponent's points remain valid. 25.2.2.2

If that moment cannot be determined, no point(s) cancellation takes place, and a point and service to the opponent is the only sanction. 6.1.3

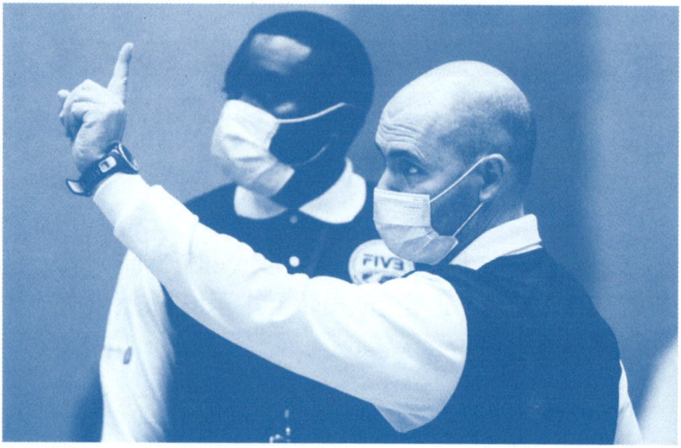

7.7 轮转错误

图 11 (13)

7.7.1 没有按照轮转次序进行发球为轮转错误，将依照程序进行如下处理： 7.6.1, 12

7.7.1.1 记录员按响蜂鸣器停止比赛，对方得 1 分并获得发球权； 6.1.3

如果因为轮转次序错误造成比赛过程中止，不管当时比赛状况如何，对方只能从这个比赛过程中得到 1 分。

7.7.1.2 队员错误的轮转次序必须被纠正。 7.6.1

7.7.2 记录员应准确地确定犯规发生的时间，从而取消该队自犯规发生后的所有得分，对方得分仍然有效。 25.2.2.2

如果不能确定该犯规发生的时间，则不取消该队所得分数，只判对方得 1 分并获得发球权。 6.1.3

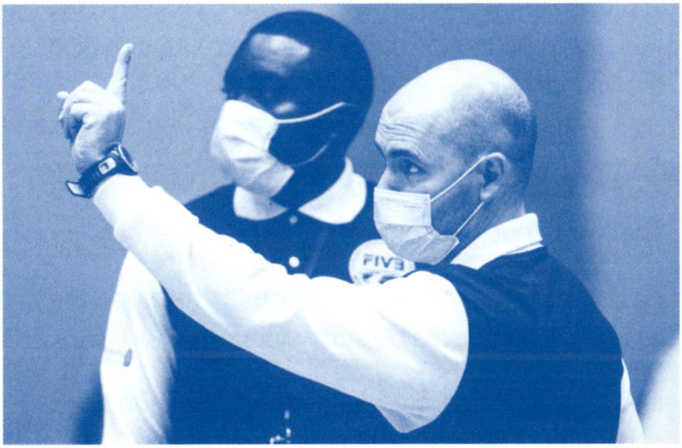

CHAPTER 4
PLAYING ACTIONS

See Rules

8 STATES OF PLAY

8.1 BALL IN PLAY

The ball is in play from the moment of the hit of the service authorized by the 1st referee. 12, 12.3

8.2 BALL OUT OF PLAY

The ball is out of play at the moment of the fault which is whistled by one of the referees; in the absence of a fault, at the moment of the whistle.

8.3 BALL "IN" D11 (14), D12 (1)

The ball is "in" if at any moment of its contact with the floor, some part of the ball touches the court, including the boundary lines. 1.1, 1.3.2

8.4 BALL "OUT"

The ball is "out" when:

8.4.1 all parts of the ball which contact the floor are completely outside the boundary lines; 1.3.2, D11 (15), D12 (2)

8.4.2 it touches an object outside the court, the ceiling or a person out of play; D11 (15), D12 (4)

第四节
比赛行为

参照规则

8　比赛的状态

8.1　进入比赛

经第 1 裁判员准许，发球队员击球为进入比赛。　12, 12.3

8.2　比赛的中止

裁判员鸣哨即为比赛的中止。如果裁判员是因出现犯规而鸣哨，则比赛的中止是由犯规一刻开始的。

8.3　界内球

图 11 (14), 图 12 (1) 1.1, 1.3.2

球的任何部分在任何时间触及比赛场区的地面（包括界线）为界内球。

8.4　界外球

下列情况为界外球：

8.4.1　球接触地面的所有部分完全在界线以外；　1.3.2, 图 11 (15), 图 12 (2)

8.4.2　球触及场外物体 、天花板或非场上比赛队员；　图 11 (15), 图 12 (4)

8.4.3 it touches the antennae, ropes, posts or the net itself outside the side bands; 2.3, D3, D5a, D11 (15), D12 (4)

8.4.4 it crosses the vertical plane of the net either partially or totally outside the crossing space (except in the case of Rule 10.1.2) ; 2.3, D5a, D5b, D11 (15), D12 (4)

8.4.5 it crosses completely the lower space under the net. 23.3.2.3f, D5a,D11 (22)

9 PLAYING THE BALL

Each team must play within its own playing area and space (except Rule 10.1.2). The ball may, however, be retrieved from beyond its own free zone and over the scoring table in its complete extension. D1b

9.1 TEAM HITS

A hit is any contact with the ball by a player in play.

The team is entitled to a maximum of three hits (in addition to blocking), for returning the ball. If more are used, the team commits the fault of "FOUR HITS". 14.4.1

9.1.1 CONSECUTIVE CONTACTS

A player may not hit the ball two times consecutively (except Rules 9.2.3, 14.2 and 14.4.2). 9.2.3, 14.2, 14.4.2

9.1.2 SIMULTANEOUS CONTACTS

Two or three players may touch the ball at the same moment.

9.1.2.1 When two (or three) team-mates touch the ball simultaneously, it is counted as two (or three) hits (with the exception of blocking). If they reach for the ball, but only one of them touches it, one hit is counted. A collision of players does not constitute a fault.

8.4.3　球触及标志杆、网绳、网柱或球网标志带外侧的部分；　2.3, 图 3, 图 5a, 图 11 (15), 图 12 (4)

8.4.4　球的部分或整体从过网区垂直平面以外过网（规则 10.1.2 除外）；　23, 图 5a, 图 5b, 图 11 (15), 图 12 (4)

8.4.5　球的整体从网下空间穿过。　23.3.2.3f, 图 5a, 图 11 (22)

9　击球

每支球队必须在其场地及空间内击球（规则 10.1.2 除外），但可以越出本方无障碍区和越过记录台及记录台的延长线将球救回。　图 1b

9.1　球队的击球

比赛中，队员与球的任何触及都被视为击球。

每队最多可击球 3 次（拦网除外）将球击回对方场区。如果超过 3 次，则该队被判为“4 次击球”。　14.4.1

9.1.1　连续击球

1 名队员不得连续击球 2 次（规则 9.2.3、14.2 和 14.4.2 除外）。　9.2.3, 14.2, 14.4.2

9.1.2　同时击球

2 名或 3 名队员可以同时触球。

9.1.2.1　同队的 2 名（或 3 名）队员同时触到球时，被记为 2 次（或 3 次）击球（拦网除外）。如果只有其中 1 名队员触球，则只记 1 次。队员之间的碰撞不算犯规。

9.1.2.2 When two opponents touch the ball simultaneously over the net and the ball remains in play, the team receiving the ball is entitled to another three hits. If such a ball goes "out", it is the fault of the team on the opposite side.

9.1.2.3 If simultaneous hits by two opponents over the net lead to an extended contact with the ball, play continues.

9.1.3 ASSISTED HIT

Within the playing area, a player is not permitted to take support from a team-mate or any structure/object in order to hit the ball. 1

However, a player who is about to commit a fault (touch the net or cross the centre line, etc.) may be stopped or held back by a team-mate. 1.3.3, 11.4.4

9.2 CHARACTERISTICS OF THE HIT

9.2.1 The ball may touch any part of the body.

9.2.2 The ball must not be caught and/or thrown. It can rebound in any direction. 9.3.3, D11 (16)

9.2.3 The ball may touch various parts of the body, provided that the contacts take place simultaneously.

Exceptions:

9.2.3.1 at blocking, consecutive contacts may be made by one or more player(s), provided that the contacts occur during one action; 14.1.1, 14.2

9.2.3.2 at the first hit of the team, the ball may contact various parts of the body consecutively, provided that the contacts occur during one action. 9.1, 14.4

9.1.2.2 2 名不同球队的队员在网上同时触球时，比赛继续进行，获球一方可再击球 3 次。如果该球落在某方场区之外，则判对方击球出界。

9.1.2.3 如果 2 名不同球队的队员在网上同时触球并造成短暂停顿，则比赛继续进行。

9.1.3 借助击球

队员不得在比赛场地之内借助同伴或任何物体的支持进行击球。 1

但是队员可以挡住或拉住另一名即将犯规（如触网、过中线等）的同队队员。 1.3.3, 11.4.4

9.2 击球的性质

9.2.1 球可以触及身体的任何部位。

9.2.2 球不能被接住或抛出。球可以向任何方向弹出。 9.3.3, 图 11 (16)

9.2.3 球可以触及身体的不同部位，但前提是同时。

下列情况除外：

9.2.3.1 拦网时，1 名或多名队员可以在一个动作中连续触球； 14.1.1, 14.2

9.2.3.2 在第 1 次击球时，允许身体不同部位在一个动作中连续触球。 9.1, 14.4

9.3 FAULTS IN PLAYING THE BALL

9.3.1 FOUR HITS: a team hits the ball four times before returning it. 9.1, D11 (18)

9.3.2 ASSISTED HIT: a player takes support from a team-mate or any structure/object in order to hit the ball within the playing area. 9.1.3

9.3.3 CATCH: the ball is caught and/or thrown; it does not rebound from the hit. 9.2.2, D11 (16)

9.3.4 DOUBLE CONTACT: a player hits the ball twice in succession or the ball contacts various parts of his/her body in succession. 9.2.3, D11 (17)

10 BALL AT THE NET

10.1 BALL CROSSING THE NET

10.1.1 The ball sent to the opponent's court must go over the net within the crossing space. The crossing space is the part of the vertical plane of the net limited as follows: 2.4, 10.2, D5a

10.1.1.1 below, by the top of the net; 2.2

10.1.1.2 at the sides, by the antennae, and their imaginary extension; 2.4

10.1.1.3 above, by the ceiling.

10.1.2 The ball that has crossed the net plane to the opponent's free zone totally or partly through the external space, may be played back within the team hits, provided that: 9.1, D5b

10.1.2.1 the opponent's court is not touched by the player; 11.2.2

10.1.2.2 the ball, when played back, crosses the net plane again totally or partly through the external space on the same side of the court. 11.4.4, D5b

9.3 击球时的犯规

9.3.1 4 次击球：一支球队连续击球 4 次。 9.1, 图 11 (18)

9.3.2 借助击球：队员在比赛场地内借助同伴或任何物体的支持进行击球。 9.1.3

9.3.3 持球：球被接住或抛出，而不是被弹击出。 9.2.2, 图 11 (16)

9.3.4 连击：1 名队员连续击球 2 次，或球连续触及 1 名队员身体的不同部位。 9.2.3, 图 11 (17)

10 球网附近的球

10.1 球通过球网

10.1.1 球必须通过球网上空的过网区进入对方场区。过网区是球网垂直平面的一部分，其范围如下： 2.4, 10.2, 图 5a

10.1.1.1 下至球网上沿； 2.2

10.1.1.2 两侧至标志杆及其延长线； 2.4

10.1.1.3 上至天花板。

10.1.2 球的整体或部分从非过网区进入对方无障碍区，可以在下列情况将球击回： 9.1, 图 5b

10.1.2.1 队员不得触及对方场区； 11.2.2

10.1.2.2 球被击回时，球的整体或部分必须从同侧的非过网区通过。 11.4.4, 图 5b

The opponent team may not prevent such action.

10.1.3 The ball that is heading towards the opponent' s court through the lower space is in play until the moment it has completely crossed the vertical plane of the net. 23.3.2.3f, D5a,D11 (22)

10.2 BALL TOUCHING THE NET

While crossing the net, the ball may touch it. 10.1.1

10.3 BALL IN THE NET

10.3.1 A ball driven into the net may be recovered within the limits of the three team hits. 9.1

10.3.2 If the ball rips the mesh of the net or tears it down, the rally is cancelled and replayed.

11 PLAYER AT THE NET

11.1 REACHING BEYOND THE NET

11.1.1 In blocking, a player may touch the ball beyond the net, provided that he/she does not interfere with the opponent' s play before the latter' s attack hit. 14.1, 14.3

11.1.2 After an attack hit, a player is permitted to pass his/her hand beyond the net, provided that the contact has been made within his/her own playing space.

11.2 PENETRATION UNDER THE NET

11.2.1 It is permitted to penetrate into the opponent' s space under the net, provided that this does not interfere with the opponent' s play.

对方队员不得阻碍此击球。

10.1.3　球从网下飞向对方场区时，球的整体越过球网下方垂直平面之前，比赛继续进行。 23.3.2.3f, 图 5a, 图 11 (22)

10.2　球触球网

球通过球网时可以触及球网。 10.1.1

10.3　球入球网

10.3.1　球入球网后，在该队 3 次击球的范围内可以再次被击出。 9.1

10.3.2　如果球击破球网或使球网坠落，该球取消并重新进行。

11　球网附近的队员

11.1　越过球网

11.1.1　拦网时允许拦网队员越过球网触球，但不得在对方进攻性击球前或击球时干扰对方。 14.1, 14.3

11.1.2　进攻性击球后，允许手过球网，但击球必须在本方场区空间。

11.2　网下穿越

11.2.1　在不干扰对方比赛的情况下，允许队员从网下穿越进入对方空间。

11.2.2 Penetration into the opponent's court, beyond the centre line: 1.3.3, 11.2.2.1, D11 (22)

11.2.2.1 to touch the opponent's court with a foot (feet) is permitted, provided that some part of the penetrating foot (feet) remains either in contact with or directly above the centre line and this action does not interfere with the opponent's play; 1.3.3, D11 (22)

11.2.2.2 to touch the opponent's court with any part of the body above the feet is permitted provided that it does not interfere with the opponent's play. 1.3.3, 11.2.2.1, D11 (22)

11.2.3 A player may enter the opponent's court after the ball goes out of play. 8.2

11.2.4 Players may penetrate into the opponent's free zone provided that they do not interfere with the opponent's play.

11.3 CONTACT WITH THE NET

11.3.1 Contact with the net by a player between the antennae, during the action of playing the ball, is a fault. 11.4.4, 23.3.2.3c, 24.3.2.3, D3

The action of playing the ball includes (among others) take-off, hit (or attempt) and landing safely, ready for a new action.

11.3.2 Players may touch the post, ropes, or any other object outside the antennae, including the net itself, provided that it does not interfere with the play (except Rule 9.1.3). D3

11.3.3 When the ball is driven into the net, causing it to touch an opponent, no fault is committed.

11.2.2　穿越中线进入对方场区：　1.3.3, 11.2.2.1, 图 11 (22)

11.2.2.1　1 只（2 只）脚触及对方场区的同时，其余部分接触中线或置于中线上空是被允许的，但此行为不得干扰对方队员击球；　1.3.3, 图 11 (22)

11.2.2.2　队员脚以上的身体任何部位触及对方场区都是被允许的，但前提是不得干扰对方比赛。　1.3.3, 11.2.2.1, 图 11 (22)

11.2.3　比赛成死球后，队员可以进入对方场区。　8.2

11.2.4　在不干扰对方比赛的情况下，队员可以进入对方无障碍区。

11.3　触网

11.3.1　队员的击球行为触及标志杆以内球网的部分为犯规。　11.4.4, 23.3.2.3c, 24.3.2.3, 图 3

击球行为包括（但不限于）起跳、击球（或试图击球）、落地至准备下一个动作。

11.3.2　队员可以触及网柱、网绳或标志杆外侧的其他任何物体，包括球网本身，但不得干扰比赛（规则 9.1.3 除外）。　图 3

11.3.3　由于球被击入球网而造成的球网触及队员的情况不算犯规。

11.4 PLAYER'S FAULTS AT THE NET

11.4.1 A player touches the ball or an opponent in the opponent's space before or during the opponent's attack hit. 11.1.1, D11 (20)

11.4.2 A player interferes with the opponent's play while penetrating into the opponent' s space under the net. 11.2.1

11.4.3 A player's foot (feet) penetrates completely into the opponent's court. 11.2.2.2, D11 (22)

11.4.4 A player interferes with play by (amongst others): D11 (19)

- touching the net between the antennae or the antenna itself during his/her action of playing the ball; 11.3.1
- using the net between the antennae as a support or stabilizing aid;
- creating an unfair advantage over the opponent by touching the net;
- making actions which hinder an opponent's legitimate attempt to play the ball;
- catching/holding on to the net.

Any player close to the ball as it is played, and who is him/herself trying to play it, is considered in the action of playing the ball, even if no contact is made with it.

However, touching the net outside the antenna is not to be considered a fault (except for Rule 9.1.3).

12 SERVICE

The service is the act of putting the ball into play, by the back-right player, placed in the service zone. 1.4.2, 8.1, 12.4.1

11.4 队员在球网附近的犯规

11.4.1 对方进攻性击球前或击球时，在对方空间内触及球或对方队员。 11.1.1, 图 11 (20)

11.4.2 从球网下方穿越进入对方空间并干扰对方比赛。 11.2.1

11.4.3 队员的单脚（双脚）全部越过中线进入对方场区。 11.2.2.2, 图 11 (22)

11.4.4 队员干扰比赛的行为涉及（但不限于）下列情况： 图 11 (19)

—击球行为触及标志杆及标志杆以内球网的任何部分； 11.3.1

—利用球网进行支撑或稳定身体；

—通过触网造成对本方有利；

—妨碍了对方合法的击球试图；

—拉住或抓住球网。

任何队员靠近球击球或准备击球时，不管他是否击到球，都被视作击球行为。

但是，队员身体触及标志杆外侧的球网不算犯规（规则 9.1.3 除外）。

12 发球

发球是由后排右侧队员在发球区内将球击出并进入比赛的行为。 1.4.2, 8.1, 12.4.1

12.1 FIRST SERVICE IN A SET

12.1.1 The first service of the first set, as well as that of the deciding 5th set is executed by the team determined by the toss. 6.3.2, 7.1

12.1.2 The other sets will be started with the service of the team that did not serve first in the previous set.

12.2 SERVICE ORDER

12.2.1 The players must follow the service order recorded on the line-up sheet. 7.3.1, 7.3.2

12.2.2 After the first service in a set, the player to serve is determined as follows: 12.1

12.2.2.1 when the serving team wins the rally, the player (or his/her substitute) who served before, serves again; 6.1.3, 15.5

12.2.2.2 when the receiving team wins the rally, it gains the right to serve and rotates before actually serving. The player who moves from the front-right position to the back-right position will serve. 6.1.3, 7.6.2

12.3 AUTHORIZATION OF THE SERVICE

The 1st referee authorizes the service, after having checked that the two teams are ready to play and that the server is in possession of the ball. 12, D11 (1)

12.4 EXECUTION OF THE SERVICE D11 (10)

12.4.1 The ball shall be hit with one hand or any part of the arm after being tossed or released from the hand(s).

12.4.2 Only one toss or release of the ball is allowed. Dribbling or moving the ball in the hands is permitted.

12.1　首先发球

12.1.1	第 1 局和第 5 局由抽签选定发球权的球队首先发球。	6.3.2, 7.1
12.1.2	其他各局由前一局未首先发球的球队首先发球。	

12.2　发球的次序

12.2.1	队员发球的次序按位置表上的顺序进行。	7.3.1, 7.3.2
12.2.2	在每一局的第一次发球后，队员按下列规定进行发球：	12.1
12.2.2.1	当发球队胜 1 球时，原发球队员（或其替补队员）继续发球；	6.1.3, 15.5
12.2.2.2	当接发球队胜 1 球时，该队获得发球权并在下一次发球前进行轮转，由前排右侧轮转至后排右侧的队员发球。	6.1.3, 7.6.2

12.3　发球的允许

	第 1 裁判员检查发球队员已持球在手，而且双方队员已做好比赛准备时，允许发球。	12, 图 11 (1)

12.4　发球的执行

图 11 (10)

12.4.1	球被抛起或持球手撤离后，必须在球落地前用一只手或手臂的任何部分将球击出。	
12.4.2	球只能被抛起或撤离手 1 次，但拍球或在手中摆弄球是被允许的。	

12.4.3 At the moment of the service hit or take-off for a jump service, the server must not touch the court (the end line included) or the floor outside the service zone. 1.4.2, 29.2.1.4, D11 (22), D12 (4)

After the hit, he/she may step or land outside the service zone, or inside the court.

12.4.4 The server must hit the ball within 8 seconds after the 1st referee whistles for service. 12.3, D11 (11)

12.4.5 A service executed before the referee's whistle is cancelled and repeated. 12.3

12.5 SCREENING

D6, D11 (12)

12.5.1 The players of the serving team must not prevent their opponent, through individual or collective screening, from seeing the service hit and the flight path of the ball. 12.5.2

12.5.2 A player or a group of players of the serving team make(s) a screen by waving arms, jumping or moving sideways during the execution of the service, or by standing grouped, in order that both the service hit and the flight path of the ball are hidden until the ball reaches the vertical plane of the net. Should either be visible to the receiving team this is not a screen. 12.4, D6

12.6 FAULTS MADE DURING THE SERVICE

12.6.1 Serving faults.

The following faults lead to a change of service even if the opponent is out of position. The server: 12.2.2.2, 12.7.1

12.6.1.1 violates the service order, 12.2

12.6.1.2 does not execute the service properly. 12.4

12.4.3 发球队员在击球时或发球起跳时，不得踏及场区（包括端线）和发球区以外的地面。 1.4.2, 29.2.1.4, 图 11 (22), 图 12 (4)

击球后，可以踏及或落在场区内或发球区以外。

12.4.4 发球队员必须在第 1 裁判员鸣哨允许发球后的 8 秒之内将球击出。 12.3, 图 D11 (11)

12.4.5 裁判员鸣哨允许发球前的发球无效，应重发。 12.3

12.5 发球掩护

图 6, 图 11 (12)

12.5.1 发球方队员不得通过个人或集体掩护行为阻挡对方观察发球队员的击球行为和球的飞行路线。 12.5.2

12.5.2 在发球击球直至球飞过球网垂直平面的过程中，发球方队员个人或集体挥臂、跳跃或侧向移动，或者密集站立遮挡发球击球行为和球的飞行路线，则构成发球掩护。但如果这些行为发生时没有导致遮挡，就不是掩护。 12.4, 图 6

12.6 发球时的犯规

12.6.1 发球犯规。

下列犯规应被判为发球犯规，即使对方位置错误。发球方队员： 12.2.2.2, 12.7.1

12.6.1.1 发球次序错误； 12.2

12.6.1.2 没有遵守“发球的执行”的规定。 12.4

12.6.2 Faults after the service hit.

After the ball has been correctly hit, the service becomes a fault (unless a player is out of position) if the ball: 12.4, 12.7.2

12.6.2.1 touches a player of the serving team or fails to cross the vertical plane of the net completely through the crossing space; 8.4.4, 8.4.5, 10.1.1, D11 (19)

12.6.2.2 goes "out"; 8.4, D11 (15)

12.6.2.3 passes over a screen. 12.5, D11 (12)

12.7 SERVING FAULTS AND POSITIONAL FAULTS

12.7.1 If the server makes a fault at the moment of the service hit (improper execution, wrong rotational order, etc.) and the opponent is out of position, it is the serving fault which is sanctioned. 7.5.1, 7.5.2, 12.6.1

12.7.2 Instead, if the execution of the service has been correct, but the service subsequently becomes faulty (goes out, goes over a screen, etc.), the positional fault has taken place first and is sanctioned. 7.5.3, 12.6.2

13 ATTACK HIT

13.1 CHARACTERISTICS OF THE ATTACK HIT 12, 14.1.1

13.1.1 All actions which direct the ball towards the opponent, with the exception of service and block, are considered as attack hits.

13.1.2 During an attack hit, tipping is permitted only if the ball is cleanly hit, and not caught or thrown. 9.2.2

12.6.2 发球击球后的犯规。

球被发出后，出现以下情况仍为发球犯规（除非位置错误）： 12.4, 12.7.2

12.6.2.1 球触及发球方队员或球的整体没有从过网区通过球网垂直平面； 8.4.4, 8.4.5, 10.1.1, 图 11 (19)

12.6.2.2 界外球； 8.4, 图 11 (15)

12.6.2.3 球越过构成发球掩护的队员。 12.5, 图 11 (12)

12.7 发球犯规与位置错误

12.7.1 如果发球犯规（不符合“发球的执行”、发球次序错误等）与对方位置错误同时发生，则判发球犯规。 7.5.1, 7.5.2, 12.6.1

12.7.2 相反，如果发球击球后的犯规（界外球、发球掩护等）与对方位置错误同时发生，则判位置错误犯规。 7.5.3, 12.6.2

13 进攻性击球

13.1 进攻性击球的特性 12, 14.1.1

13.1.1 除发球和拦网外，所有直接朝向对方的击球都是进攻性击球。

13.1.2 进攻性击球时，只有当球被明确地击出，吊球才被允许，同时不得接住或抛出球。 9.2.2

13.1.3 An attack hit is completed at the moment the ball completely crosses the vertical plane of the net or is touched by an opponent.

13.2 RESTRICTIONS OF THE ATTACK HIT

13.2.1 A front-row player may complete an attack hit at any height, provided that the contact with the ball has been made within the player's own playing space (except Rules 13.2.4 and 13.3.6). 7.4.1.1

13.2.2 A back-row player may complete an attack hit at any height from behind the front zone: 1.4.1, 7.4.1.2, 19.3.1.2, D8

13.2.2.1 at his/her take-off, the player's foot (feet) must neither have touched nor crossed over the attack line; 1.3.4

13.2.2.2 after his/her hit, the player may land within the front zone. 1.4.1

13.2.3 A back-row player may also complete an attack hit from the front zone, if at the moment of the contact a part of the ball is lower than the top of the net. 1.4.1, 7.4.1.2, D8

13.2.4 No player is permitted to complete an attack hit on the OPPONENT' S service, when the ball is in the front zone and entirely higher than the top of the net. 1.4.1

13.3 FAULTS OF THE ATTACK HIT

13.3.1 A player hits the ball within the playing space of the opposing team. 13.2.1, D11 (20)

13.3.2 A player hits the ball "out". 8.4, D11 (15)

13.3.3 A back-row player completes an attack hit from the front zone, if at the moment of the hit the ball is entirely higher than the top of the net. 1.4.1, 7.4.1.2, 13.2.3, D11 (21)

13.1.3	球的整体通过球网垂直平面或触及对方队员时，被认为完成进攻性击球。	

13.2 进攻性击球的限制

13.2.1	前排队员可以对任何高度的球完成进攻性击球，但触球时必须在本方场区空间内（规则 13.2.4、13.3.6 除外）。	7.4.1.1
13.2.2	后排队员可以在前场区后对任何高度的球完成进攻性击球，但是：	1.4.1, 7.4.1.2, 19.3.1.2, 图 8
13.2.2.1	起跳时脚不得踏及或越过进攻线；	1.3.4
13.2.2.2	击球后可以落在前场区。	1.4.1
13.2.3	后排队员也可以在前场区完成进攻性击球，但触球时球的一部分必须低于球网上沿。	1.4.1, 7.4.1.2, 图 8
13.2.4	接发球队的队员不得在前场区内对高于球网上沿的对方发球进行进攻性击球。	1.4.1

13.3 进攻性击球的犯规

13.3.1	队员在对方空间内击球。	13.2.1, 图 11 (20)
13.3.2	队员击球出界。	8.4, 图 11 (15)
13.3.3	后排队员在前场区完成进攻性击球，并且击球时球的整体高于球网上沿。	1.4.1, 7.4.1.2, 13.2.3, 图 11 (21)

13.3.4 A player completes an attack hit on the opponent's service, when the ball is in the front zone and entirely higher than the top of the net. 1.4.1, 13.2.4, D11 (21)

13.3.5 A Libero completes an attack hit if at the moment of the hit the ball is entirely higher than the top of the net. 19.3.1.2, 23.3.2.3d, D11 (21)

13.3.6 A player completes an attack hit from higher than the top of the net when the ball is coming from an overhand finger pass by a Libero in his/her front zone. 1.4.1, 19.3.1.4, 23.3.2.3e, D11 (21)

14 BLOCK

14.1 BLOCKING

14.1.1 Blocking is the action of players close to the net to intercept the ball coming from the opponent by reaching higher than the top of the net, regardless of the height of the ball contact. Only front-row players are permitted to complete a block, but at the moment of the contact with the ball, a part of the body must be higher than the top of the net. 7.4.1.1

14.1.2 Block attempt

A block attempt is the action of blocking without touching the ball.

14.1.3 Completed block

A block is completed whenever the ball is touched by a blocker. D7

14.1.4 Collective block

A collective block is executed by two or three players close to each other and is completed when one of them touches the ball.

13.3.4 队员在前场区内对高于球网上沿的对方发球完成进攻性击球。 1.4.1, 13.2.4, 图 11 (21)

13.3.5 自由防守队员对高于球网上沿的球完成进攻性击球。 19.3.1.2, 23.3.2.3d, 图 11 (21)

13.3.6 当自由防守队员在前场区用上手传出球后，本方队员在高于球网处完成进攻性击球。 1.4.1, 19.3.1.4, 23.3.2.3e, 图 11 (21)

14 拦网

14.1 拦网行为

14.1.1 拦网行为是队员靠近球网，在高于球网处阻挡对方来球的行动，与触球点的高度无关。只有前排队员被允许完成拦网，但在触球时，其身体必须有一部分高于球网上沿。 7.4.1.1

14.1.2 拦网试图

没有触及球的拦网行动为拦网试图。

14.1.3 完成拦网

触及球的拦网行动为完成拦网。 图 7

14.1.4 集体拦网

2 名或 3 名队员彼此靠近进行拦网的行动为集体拦网，其中 1 人触球即为完成拦网。

14.2 BLOCK CONTACT

Consecutive (quick and continuous) contacts with the ball may occur by one or more blockers, provided that the contacts are made during one action. 9.1.1, 9.2.3

14.3 BLOCKING WITHIN THE OPPONENT'S SPACE D11 (20)

In blocking, the player may place his/her hands and arms beyond the net, provided that this action does not interfere with the opponent's play. Thus, it is not permitted to touch the ball beyond the net before an opponent has executed an attack hit. 13.1.1

14.4 BLOCK AND TEAM HITS

14.4.1 A block contact is not counted as a team hit. Consequently, after a block contact, a team is entitled to three hits to return the ball. 9.1, 14.4.2 14.4.1

14.4.2 The first hit after the block may be executed by any player, including the one who has touched the ball during the block.

14.5 BLOCKING THE SERVICE 12, D11 (12)

To block an opponent's service is forbidden.

14.6 BLOCKING FAULTS D11 (20)

14.6.1 The blocker touches the ball in the OPPONENT'S space before the opponent's attack hit. 14.3

14.6.2 A back-row player or a Libero completes a block or participates in a completed block. 14.1, 14.5, 19.3.1.3

14.6.3 Blocking the opponent's service. 14.5, D11 (12)

14.2　拦网触球

在一个动作中，球可以连续（迅速而连贯地）触及 1 名或更多名拦网队员。 9.1.1, 9.2.3

14.3　在对方空间内拦网

图 11 (20)

拦网时，队员可以将手或手臂伸过球网，但不得干扰对方击球。不允许在对方进攻性击球之前进行过网拦网的触球。 13.1.1

14.4　拦网与球队的击球

14.4.1　拦网的触球不算作球队 3 次击球中的 1 次。因此，拦网触球后该队还可以击球 3 次。 9.1, 14.4.2

14.4.1

14.4.2　拦网后可以由任何一名队员进行第 1 次击球，包括拦网时已经触球的队员。

14.5　拦发球

12, 图 11 (12)

拦对方的发球是被禁止的。

14.6　拦网犯规

图 11 (20)

14.6.1　拦网队员于对方进攻性击球前在对方场地空间内触球。 14.3

14.6.2　后排队员或自由防守队员完成拦网或参与了拦网的完成。 14.1, 14.5, 19.3.1.3

14.6.3　拦对方的发球。 14.5, 图 11 (12)

14.6.4 The ball is sent "out" off the block. 8.4

14.6.5 Blocking the ball in the opponent's space from outside the antenna.

14.6.6 A Libero attempts an individual or collective block. 14.1.1, 19.3.1.3

14.6.4　拦网出界。 8.4

14.6.5　从标志杆外侧伸入对方空间拦网。

14.6.6　自由防守队员试图进行个人拦网或参加集体拦网。 14.1.1, 19.3.1.3

CHAPTER 5

INTERRUPTIONS, DELAYS AND INTERVALS

See Rules

15 INTERRUPTIONS

An interruption is the time between one completed rally and the 1st referee' s whistle for the next service. 6.1.3, 8.1, 8.2,15.4, 15.5,24.2.6

The only **regular game** interruptions are TIME-OUTS and SUBSTITUTIONS.

15.1 NUMBER OF REGULAR GAME INTERRUPTIONS

Each team may request a maximum of two time-outs and six substitutions per set. 6.2, 15.4, 15.5

15.2 SEQUENCE OF REGULAR GAME INTERRUPTIONS

15.2.1 Request for one or two time-outs, and one request for substitution by either team may follow one another, within the same interruption. 15.4, 15.5

15.2.2 However, a team is not authorized to make consecutive requests for substitution during the same interruption. Two or more players may be substituted at the same time within the same request. 15.5, 15.6.1

15.2.3 There must be a completed rally between two separate substitution requests by the same team. [Exception: a forced substitution due to injury or expulsion/ disqualification (15.5.2, 15.7, 15.8)]. 6.1.3, 15.5

第五节

比赛间断与延误比赛

参照规则

15 间断

间断是在一个完整的比赛过程结束后至下一次第 1 裁判员鸣哨发球之前的时间。 6.1.3, 8.1, 8.2,15.4, 15.5,24.2.6

合法比赛间断只有“暂停”和“换人”。

15.1 合法比赛间断的次数

每局比赛中，每支球队最多可以请求 2 次暂停和 6 人次换人。 6.2, 15.4, 15.5

15.2 合法比赛间断的次序

15.2.1 在同一次比赛间断中，可以请求 1 或 2 次暂停，一支球队请求换人后，另一支球队也可以请求换人。 15.4, 15.5

15.2.2 在同一次比赛间断中，同一支球队不得连续提出换人请求。但在同一次换人请求中，可以同时替换 2 名或多名队员。 15.5, 15.6.1

15.2.3 同一支球队再次请求换人时，必须经过一次完整的比赛过程 [因受伤或被判罚出场或被取消比赛资格的被迫替换除外 (规则 15.5.2、15.7、15.8)]。 6.1.3, 15.5

15.2.4 It is not permitted to request any regular game interruption after having had a request rejected and sanctioned by a delay warning during the same interruption (i.e. before the end of next completed rally). 16.1.2

15.3 REQUEST FOR REGULAR GAME INTERRUPTIONS

15.3.1 Regular game interruptions may be requested by the coach, or in the absence of the coach, by the assistant coach or by the game captain, and only by them. 5.1.2.3, 5.2.3.3, 5.3.2, 15

15.3.2 Substitution before the start of a set is permitted, and should be recorded as a regular substitution in that set. 7.3.4

15.4 TIME-OUTS

15.4.1 Time-out requests must be made by showing the corresponding hand signal, when the ball is out of play and before the whistle for service. All requested time-outs last for 30 seconds. 6.1.3, 8.2, 12.3, D11 (4)

For FIVB, World and Official Competitions the length of the Time–outs could be adjusted if the FIVB approves such request based on the request from the organizer.

For FIVB, World and Official Competitions it is obligatory to use the buzzer and then the hand signal to request time–out.

15.4.2 During all time-outs, the players in play must go to the free zone near their bench. D1a

15.5 SUBSTITUTION

15.5.1 A substitution is the act by which a player, other than the Libero or his/her replacement player, after being recorded by the scorer, enters the game to occupy the position of another player, who must leave the court at that moment. 19.3.2.1, D11 (5)

15.2.4 在同一次比赛间断中（即在下一个完整比赛过程结束前），当一次请求被拒绝后和受到延误警告判罚后，不允许再次请求比赛间断。 16.1.2

15.3 请求合法比赛间断

15.3.1 只有教练员可以请求合法的比赛间断；当教练员缺席时，则只能由该队助理教练员或场上队长提出。 5.1.2.3, 5.2.3.3, 5.3.2, 15

15.3.2 每局开始前请求换人是被允许的，但应计算在该局正常换人的次数之内。 7.3.4

15.4 暂停

15.4.1 请求暂停必须在比赛成死球后至裁判员鸣哨允许发球前进行，并使用相应手势。所有被请求的暂停时间均为 30 秒。 6.1.3, 8.2, 12.3, 图 11 (4)

国际排联（FIVB）比赛、世界性比赛和正式比赛中，暂停时长可以根据组委会的请求经国际排联（FIVB）批准后进行调整。

国际排联（FIVB）比赛、世界性比赛和正式比赛中，必须使用蜂鸣器然后做出手势请求暂停。

15.4.2 所有暂停期间，比赛队员必须前往该队球队席附近的无障碍区。 图 1a

15.5 换人

15.5.1 一名队员离开比赛场地，并由另一名队员经记录员登记后占据其位置的行为称为换人（自由防守队员的替换除外）。 19.3.2.1, 图 11 (5)

15.5.2 When the substitution is enforced through injury to a player in play this may be accompanied by the coach (or game captain) showing the corresponding hand signal. 5.1.2.3, 5.2.3.3, 6.1.3, 8.2, 12.3, D11 (5)

15.6 LIMITATION OF SUBSTITUTIONS

15.6.1 A player of the starting line-up may leave the game, but only once in a set, and re-enter, but only once in a set, and only to his/her previous position in the line-up. 7.3.1

15.6.2 A substitute player may enter the game in place of a player of the starting line-up, but only once per set, and he/she can only be substituted by the same starting player. 7.3.1

15.7 EXCEPTIONAL SUBSTITUTION

A player (except the Libero) who cannot continue playing due to injury/illness, or expulsion/disqualification should be substituted legally. If this is not possible, the team is entitled to make an EXCEPTIONAL substitution, beyond the limits of Rule 15.6. 15.6, 19.4.3, 21.3.2, 21.3.3, D11 (5)

An exceptional substitution means that any player who is not on the court at the time of the injury/illness/expulsion/disqualification, except the Libero, second Libero or their regular replacement player, may be substituted into the game for the injured/ill/expelled/disqualified player. The injured/ill/expelled player substituted via exceptional substitution is not allowed to re-enter the match.

An exceptional substitution cannot be counted in any case as a regular substitution, but should be recorded on the score sheet as part of the total of substitutions in the set and the match.

15.5.2　当一名受伤队员被进行特殊换人时，教练员（或场上队长）须做出换人手势。　5.1.2.3, 5.2.3.3, 6.1.3, 8.2, 12.3, 图 11 (5)

15.6　换人的限制

15.6.1　每局首发阵容中的队员，在同一局中可以退出比赛和再上场比赛各 1 次，而且只能回到原阵容的位置。　7.3.1

15.6.2　替补队员每局只能上场比赛 1 次替换首发阵容中的队员，而且他只能由被他替换下场的队员来替换。　7.3.1

15.7　特殊换人

一名队员（自由防守队员除外）因受伤、生病或被判罚出场、被取消比赛资格而不能继续比赛时，应当进行合法换人。如不能进行该换人，球队可采用超出规则 15.6 限制的“特殊换人”。　15.6, 19.4.3, 21.3.2, 21.3.3, 图 11 (5)

特殊换人是指受伤、生病、被判罚出场、被取消比赛资格发生时，不在场上的队员（自由防守队员、第 2 自由防守队员或由他们替换的队员除外）可以替换受伤、生病、被判罚出场、被取消比赛资格的队员。通过特殊换人被换下场的受伤、生病、被判罚出场的队员不得重新上场比赛。

在任何情况下，特殊换人都不作为换人的次数计算，但应登记在记录表上作为本局和本场比赛换人总数的一部分。

15.8 SUBSTITUTION FOR EXPULSION OR DISQUALIFICATION

An "EXPELLED" or "DISQUALIFIED" player must be substituted immediately through a legal substitution. If this is not possible, the team has the right to do an exceptional substitution. If this is not possible, the team is declared "INCOMPLETE". 6.4.3, 7.3.1, 15.6, 15.7, 21.3.2, 21.3.3, D11 (5)

15.9 ILLEGAL SUBSTITUTION

15.9.1 A substitution is illegal, if it exceeds the limitations indicated in Rule 15.6 (except the case of Rule 15.7), or an unregistered player is involved.

15.9.2 When a team has made an illegal substitution and the play has been resumed the following procedure shall apply, in sequence: 8.1, 15.6

15.9.2.1 the team is penalized with a point and service to the opponent; 6.1.3

15.9.2.2 the substitution must be rectified;

15.9.2.3 the points scored by the team at fault since the fault was committed are cancelled; the opponent's points remain valid.

15.10 SUBSTITUTION PROCEDURE

15.10.1 Substitution must be carried out within the substitution zone. 1.4.3, D1b

15.10.2 A substitution shall only last the time needed for recording the substitution on the score sheet, and allowing entry and exit of the players. 15.10, 24.2.6, 25.2.2.3

15.8　被判罚出场或被取消比赛资格的换人

队员被“判罚出场”或“取消比赛资格”后，须立即进行合法换人。如不能进行该换人，球队可申请进行特殊换人。如该换人也不能进行，则该队被宣布为“阵容不完整”。 6.4.3, 7.3.1, 15.6, 15.7, 21.3.2, 21.3.3, 图 11 (5)

15.9　不合法的换人

15.9.1　不合法的换人是超出规则 15.6 限制 (规则 15.7 的情况除外) 或涉及没有进行登记的队员的换人。

15.9.2　一支球队进行了不合法的换人，而且比赛已重新开始，应按如下步骤进行处理： 8.1, 15.6

15.9.2.1　判该队失 1 分、由对方发球； 6.1.3

15.9.2.2　对不合法的换人给予纠正；

15.9.2.3　取消该队在此犯规中所得的分数，对方得分仍然保留。

15.10　换人的程序

15.10.1　换人必须在换人区内进行。 1.4.3, 图 1b

15.10.2　换人时所持续的时间仅限记录员登记和队员进出场必需的时间。 15.10, 24.2.6, 25.2.2.3

15.10.3.1 The actual request for substitution starts at the moment of the entrance of the substitute player(s) into the substitution zone, ready to play, during an interruption. The coach does not need to make a substitution hand signal except if the substitution is for injury or before the start of the set.

15.10.3.2 If the player is not ready in the moment of the request, the substitution is not granted and the team is sanctioned for a delay. 16.2, D9

15.10.3.3 The request for substitution is acknowledged and announced by the scorer or 2nd referee, by use of the buzzer or whistle respectively. The 2nd referee authorises the substitution. 24.2.6

For FIVB, World and Official Competitions, numbered paddles are used to facilitate the substitution (except when electronic devices are used to transmit the data to the scorer).

15.10.4 If a team intends to make simultaneously more than one substitution, all substitute players must enter the substitution zone at the same time to be considered in the same request. In this case, substitutions must be made in succession, one pair of players after another. If one is illegal, the legal one(s) is/are granted and the illegal is rejected and subject to a delay sanction. 1.4.3, 15.2.2

15.11 IMPROPER REQUESTS

15.11.1 It is improper to request any regular game interruption: 15

15.11.1.1 during a rally or at the moment of or after the whistle to serve, 12.3

*15.10.3.1 场外队员在比赛间断时只要进入了换人区，并且做好了上场的一切准备，就是提出了换人的请求。此时，除队员受伤或局前的替换之外，教练员不必做出换人手势。

15.10.3.2 提出换人请求时，如队员没有做好准备，则该请求应被拒绝并判为一次延误。 16.2, 图 9

15.10.3.3 记录员或第 2 裁判员分别使用蜂鸣器或哨音确认和宣告换人的请求。由第 2 裁判员负责换人的程序。 24.2.6

国际排联（FIVB）比赛、世界性比赛和正式比赛中，队员换人时须使用换人牌（提供电子设备用于换人请求的情况除外）。

15.10.4 如果一支球队在同一间断中想替换 1 名以上的队员，则所有请求上场的队员都必须进入换人区。替换时，队员一对对相继进行。如其中有不合法的替换，必须予以拒绝并给予延误处罚。 1.4.3, 15.2.2

15.11 不符合规定的请求

15.11.1 下列情况为不符合规定的比赛间断请求： 15

15.11.1.1 在比赛进行中或在裁判员鸣哨允许发球之时（或之后）提出请求； 12.3

* 译者注：英文原文中无 15.10.3，为保持一致性，不做修改。

15.11.1.2 by a non-authorized team member, 5.1.2.3, 5.2.3.3

15.11.1.3 for a second substitution by the same team during the same interruption(i.e. before the end of the next completed rally), except in the case of injury/illness/expulsion/disqualification of a player in play, 15.2.2, 15.2.3, 15.8, 16.1, 25.2.2.6

15.11.1.4 after having exhausted the authorized number of time-outs and substitutions. 15.1

15.11.2 The first improper request by a team in the match that does not affect or delay the game shall be rejected, but it must be recorded on the score sheet without any other consequences. 16.1, 25.2.2.6

15.11.3 Any further improper request in the match by the same team constitutes a delay. 16.1.4, D11 (25)

16 GAME DELAYS

16.1 TYPES OF DELAYS

An improper action of a team that defers resumption of the game is a delay and includes, among others:

16.1.1 delaying regular game interruptions; 15.10.2

16.1.2 prolonging interruptions, after having been instructed to resume the game; 15

16.1.3 requesting an illegal substitution; 15.9

16.1.4 repeating an improper request; 15.11.3

16.1.5 delaying the game by a team member.

15.11.1.2 无请求权的成员提出请求； 5.1.2.3, 5.2.3.3

15.11.1.3 同一支球队在同一个比赛间断中（即在下一完整比赛过程结束前）再次请求换人，除非是队员受伤、生病、被判罚出场、被取消比赛资格； 15.2.2, 15.2.3, 15.8, 16.1, 25.2.2.6

15.11.1.4 超过规定的正常暂停和换人次数的请求。 15.1

15.11.2 球队在比赛中第1次出现不影响和延误比赛的不符合规定的请求时，应给予拒绝而不进行处罚，但必须登记在记录表中。 16.1, 25.2.2.6

15.11.3 同一支球队在比赛中再次提出不符合规定的请求都应被判为延误犯规。 16.1.4, 图 11 (25)

16 延误比赛

16.1 延误比赛的类型

一支球队拖延比赛继续进行的不当行为是延误比赛，这包括（但不限于）：

16.1.1 拖延正常比赛间断； 15.10.2

16.1.2 在裁判员鸣哨恢复比赛后拖延间断时间； 15

16.1.3 请求不合法的换人； 15.9

16.1.4 再次提出不符合规定的请求； 15.11.3

16.1.5 球队成员拖延比赛继续进行。

16.2 DELAY SANCTIONS D9

16.2.1 "Delay warning" and "delay penalty" are team sanctions.

16.2.1.1 Delay sanctions remain in force for the entire match. 6.3

16.2.1.2 All delay sanctions are recorded on the score sheet. 25.2.2.6

16.2.2 The first delay in the match by a team member is sanctioned with a "DELAY WARNING". 4.1.1, D11 (25)

16.2.3 The second and subsequent delays of any type by any member of the same team in the same match constitute a fault and are sanctioned with a "DELAY PENALTY": a point and service to the opponent. 6.1.3, D11 (25)

16.2.4 Delay sanctions imposed before or between sets are applied in the following set. 18.1

17 EXCEPTIONAL GAME INTERRUPTIONS

17.1 INJURY/ ILLNESS 8.1

17.1.1 Should a serious accident occur while the ball is in play, the referee must stop the game immediately and permit medical assistance to enter the court.

The rally is then replayed. 6.1.3

17.1.2 If an injured/ill player cannot be substituted legally or exceptionally, the player is given a 3-minute recovery time, but not more than once for the same player in the match. 15.6, 15.7, 24.2.8

If the player does not recover, his/her team is declared incomplete. 6.4.3, 7.3.1

16.2　对延误比赛的处罚

图 9

16.2.1　“延误警告”和“延误判罚”是对全队延误比赛行为的处罚。

16.2.1.1　延误比赛的处罚对全场比赛有效。　6.3

16.2.1.2　所有延误比赛的处罚都应被登记在记录表上。　25.2.2.6

16.2.2　在一场比赛中，对一支球队成员的第 1 次延误比赛行为给予“延误警告”。　4.1.1, 图 11 (25)

16.2.3　在一场比赛中，同一队的任何成员造成不论任何类型的第 2 次及其后的延误比赛行为，都给予“延误判罚”，失 1 分并由对方发球。　6.1.3, 图 11 (25)

16.2.4　局前和局间的延误比赛处罚记录在下一局比赛中。　18.1

17　例外的比赛中断

17.1　受伤或生病

8.1

17.1.1　比赛中出现严重伤害事故时，裁判员应该立即中断比赛，并允许医务人员进入场地。

该球重新进行。　6.1.3

17.1.2　如果受伤或生病的队员已不能进行合法换人和特殊换人，则给予该队员 3 分钟的恢复时间。在一场比赛中，同一名队员只能给予 1 次可供恢复的时间。　15.6, 15.7, 24.2.8

如果该队员不能恢复，则该队被宣布为阵容不完整。　6.4.3, 7.3.1

17.2 EXTERNAL INTERFERENCE

If there is any external interference during the game, the play has to be stopped and the rally is replayed. 6.1.3, D11 (23)

17.3 PROLONGED INTERRUPTIONS

17.3.1 If unforeseen circumstances interrupt the match, the 1st referee, the organizer and the Control Committee, if there is one, shall decide the measures to be taken to re-establish normal conditions. 23.2.3

17.3.2 Should one or several interruptions occur, not exceeding 4 hours in total: 17.3.1

17.3.2.1 if the match is resumed on the same playing court, the interrupted set shall continue normally with the same score, players (except expelled or disqualified ones) and positions. The sets already played will keep their scores; 1, 7.3

17.3.2.2 if the match is resumed on another playing court, the interrupted set is cancelled and replayed with the same team members and the same starting line-ups (except expelled or disqualified ones) and the record of all sanctions will be maintained. The sets already played will keep their scores. 7.3, 21.4.1, D9

17.3.3 Should one or several interruptions occur, exceeding 4 hours in total, the whole match shall be replayed.

18 INTERVALS AND CHANGE OF COURTS

18.1 INTERVALS

An interval is the time between sets. All intervals last three minutes. 4.2.4

17.2 外因造成的比赛中断

比赛中出现任何外界干扰，都应停止比赛，该球重新进行。 6.1.3, 图 11 (23)

17.3 被拖延的间断

17.3.1 任何意外情况阻碍比赛继续进行时，第 1 裁判员、比赛组织者和管委会成员（如有）应负责采取措施恢复比赛。 23.2.3

17.3.2 1 次或数次间断的时间累计不超过 4 小时： 17.3.1

17.3.2.1 如果比赛仍在原场地进行，则间断的一局应保持原比分、原队员（被判罚出场和取消比赛资格者除外）和原场上位置，已结束的各局比分均保留； 1, 7.3

17.3.2.2 如果比赛改在其他场地进行，则间断的一局应取消，但保持该局开始时的队员阵容（被判罚出场和取消比赛资格者除外）重新比赛，已登记的所有警告与处罚均有效，已结束的各局比分均保留。 7.3, 21.4.1, 图 9

17.3.3 1 次或数次间断的时间累计超过 4 小时，则全场比赛应重新进行。

18 局间休息与交换场区

18.1 局间休息

局间休息是两局比赛之间的时间。所有局间休息的时间均为 3 分钟。 4.2.4

During this period of time, the change of courts and line-up registrations of the teams on the score sheet are made. 7.3.2, 18.2, 25.2.1.2

The interval between the second and the third set can be extended up to 10 minutes by the competent body at the request of the organizer.

18.2 CHANGE OF COURTS D11 (3)

18.2.1 After each set, the teams change courts, with the exception of the deciding set. 7.1

18.2.2 In the deciding set, once the leading team reaches 8 points, the teams change courts without delay and the player positions remain the same. 6.3.2, 7.4.1, 25.2.2.5

If the change is not made once the leading team reaches 8 points, it will take place as soon as the error is noticed. The score at the time that the change is made remains the same.

局间休息用于交换场区和在记录表上登记球队的阵容。 7.3.2, 18.2, 25.2.1.2

应比赛主办者或组织者的要求，第 2、第 3 局之间的休息时间可延长至 10 分钟。

18.2　交换场区

图 11 (3)

18.2.1　每局结束后，两支比赛球队交换场区，决胜局除外。 7.1

18.2.2　决胜局中一支球队获得 8 分时两队交换场区，不休息，队员保持交换前的位置继续比赛。 6.3.2, 7.4.1, 25.2.2.5

如果未能及时交换场区，则应在发现此错误时立即交换，保留交换场区时两队已得比分。

CHAPTER 6

THE LIBERO PLAYER

See Rules

19 THE LIBERO PLAYER

19.1 DESIGNATION OF THE LIBERO 5

19.1.1 Each team has the right to designate from the list of players on the score sheet up to two specialist defensive players: Liberos. 4.1.1

In FIVB, World and Official competitions for Seniors, if a team has more than 12 players recorded in the score sheet, TWO Liberos are mandatory in the team list.

19.1.2 All Liberos must be recorded on the score sheet in the special lines reserved for this. 5.2.2, 25.2.1.1, 28.2.1.1

19.1.3 The Libero on court is the Acting Libero. If there is another Libero, he/she is the second Libero for the team.

Only one Libero may be on court at any time.

19.2 EQUIPMENT 4.3

The Libero player(s) must wear a uniform (or jacket/bib for the redesignated Libero) which has a different dominant colour from any colour of the rest of the team. The uniform must clearly contrast with the rest of the team. Both Liberos can be in uniforms different from each other and from the rest of the team.

第六节
自由防守队员

参照规则

19　自由防守队员

19.1　自由防守队员的指定　5

19.1.1　每支球队都有权从记录表上登记的队员名单中指定最多两名特殊的防守队员，即“自由防守队员”。　4.1.1

国际排联（FIVB）比赛、世界性比赛和正式比赛的成年比赛中，如果记录表登记的队员人数超过 12 人，则名单中必须有 2 名自由防守队员。

19.1.2　所有自由防守队员都必须在比赛前登记在记录表规定的位置中。　5.2.2, 25.2.1.1, 28.2.1.1

19. 1.3　在场上的自由防守队员是场上自由防守队员。如果该队还有另外 1 名自由防守队员，则其成为第 2 自由防守队员。

无论任何时候，场上只有 1 名自由防守队员。

19.2　装备　4.3

自由防守队员服装的主体颜色（或为新指定自由防守队员准备的背心）必须与该队其他队员服装的主体颜色形成鲜明对比。两名自由防守队员可以穿着不同于彼此和该队其他队员的服装。

The Libero uniforms must be numbered like the rest of the team.

For FIVB, World and Official competitions, the re-designated Libero should, if possible, wear the same style and colour of jersey as the original Libero, but should keep his/her own number.

19.3 ACTIONS INVOLVING THE LIBERO

19.3.1 The playing actions:

19.3.1.1 The Libero is allowed to replace any player in a back row position. 7.4.1.2

19.3.1.2 He/she is restricted to perform as a back row player and is not allowed to complete an attack hit from anywhere (including playing court and free zone) if at the moment of the contact the ball is entirely higher than the top of the net. 13.2.2, 13.2.3, 13.3.5

19.3.1.3 He/she may not serve, block or attempt to block. 12.4.1, 14.6.2, 14.6.6, D11 (12)

19.3.1.4 A player may not complete an attack hit when the ball is entirely higher than the top of the net, if the ball is coming from an overhand finger pass by a Libero in his/her front zone. The ball may be freely attacked if the Libero makes the same action from outside his/her front zone. 1.4.1, 13.3.6, 23.3.2.3d, e, D1b

19.3.2 Libero Replacements

19.3.2.1 Libero Replacements are not counted as substitutions. 6.1.3, 15.5

They are unlimited but there must be a completed rally between two Libero replacements (unless a penalty causes the team to rotate and the Libero to move to position four, or the Acting Libero becomes unable to play, making the rally incomplete.)

自由防守队员的服装必须使用与其他队员制式一致的号码。

国际排联（FIVB）比赛、世界性比赛和正式比赛中，如果可能，则新指定的自由防守队员应与原自由防守队员的服装颜色一致，但应使用自己的原服装号码。

19.3　自由防守队员涉及的行为

19.3.1　比赛行为：

19.3.1.1　自由防守队员可以替换在后排的任何一名队员。　7.4.1.2

19.3.1.2　作为受限制的后排队员，他不可以在任何位置（包括场区和无障碍区）完成球整体高于球网上沿的进攻性击球。　13.2.2, 13.2.3, 13.3.5

19.3.1.3　他不能进行发球、拦网和拦网试图。　12.4.1, 14.6.2, 14.6.6, 图 11 (12)

19.3.1.4　如果自由防守队员在前场区进行上手传球，其他队员在该球整体高于球网上沿的情况下不能进行进攻性击球，但同样的传球行为发生在进攻区之外则无妨。　1.4.1, 13.3.6, 23.3.2.3d, e, 图 1b

19.3.2　自由防守队员的替换：

19.3.2.1　涉及自由防守队员的替换不计算在换人次数之内。　6.1.3, 15.5

自由防守队员的替换不受次数限制，但涉及一名自由防守队员的两次替换时，之间必须经过一次完整的比赛过程（一次处罚造成自由防守队员轮转到 4 号位或因场上自由防守队员受伤使比赛过程不完整的情况除外）。

19.3.2.2	The regular replacement player may replace and be replaced by either Libero. The Acting Libero can only be replaced by the regular replacement player for that position or by the second Libero.	
19.3.2.3	At the start of each set, the Libero cannot enter the court until the 2nd referee has checked the line-up and authorised a Libero replacement with a starting player.	7.3.2, 12.1
19.3.2.4	Other Libero replacements must only take place while the ball is out of play and before the whistle for service.	8.2, 12.3
19.3.2.5	A Libero replacement made after the whistle for service but before the service hit should not be rejected; however, at the end of the rally, the game captain must be informed that this is not a permitted procedure, and that repetition will be subject to delay sanctions.	12.3, 12.4, D9
19.3.2.6	Subsequent late Libero replacements shall result in the play being interrupted immediately, and the imposition of a delay sanction. The team to serve next will be determined by the level of the delay sanction.	16.2, D9
19.3.2.7	The Libero and the replacing player may only enter or leave the court through the Libero Replacement Zone.	1.4.4, D1b
19.3.2.8	Libero replacements must be recorded in the Libero Control Sheet (if one is used) or on the electronic score sheet.	28.2.2.1, 28.2.2.2
19.3.2.9	An illegal Libero replacement can involve (amongst others)	
	– no completed rally between Libero replacements,	6.1.3
	– the Libero being replaced by a player other than the second Libero or the regular replacement player.	15.9

19.3.2.2 场上队员可以被任何自由防守队员替换，场上自由防守队员可以由原场上队员替换，也可以由第 2 自由防守队员替换。

19.3.2.3 每局比赛开始时，自由防守队员在第 2 裁判员核对场上位置后才能进场进行替换。 7.3.2, 12.1

19.3.2.4 其他自由防守队员的替换必须在成死球之后、裁判员鸣哨发球之前进行。 8.2, 12.3

19.3.2.5 若替换发生在鸣哨之后、击球之前可以不予拒绝，但此行为不属于合法程序，必须在该轮次结束时提醒场上队长，若再次发生则给予该队延误处罚。 12.3, 12.4, 图 9

19.3.2.6 对于再次发生的延误替换，应立即中断比赛，给予延误处罚，并由延误处罚的等级决定发球权。 16.2, 图 9

19.3.2.7 自由防守队员替换时，其上、下场的地点只能在“自由防守队员替换区”。 1.4.4, 图 1b

19.3.2.8 所有涉及自由防守队员的替换都必须在自由防守队员管理表上做记录或登记在电子记录表（如果使用）上。 28.2.2.1, 28.2.2.2

19.3.2.9 不合法的自由防守队员替换涉及（但不限于此）

—自由防守队员的替换没有经过完整的比赛过程； 6.1.3

—自由防守队员被不是原场上队员或第 2 自由防守队员的其他队员替换； 15.9

An illegal Libero replacement should be considered in the same way as an illegal substitution: 15.9

i.e. should the illegal Libero replacement be noticed before the start of the next rally, then this is corrected by the referees, and the team is sanctioned for delay; D9

should the illegal Libero replacement be noticed after the service hit, the consequences are the same as for an illegal substitution. 15.9

19.4 RE-DESIGNATION OF A NEW LIBERO

19.4.1 The Libero **becomes** unable to play if injured, ill, expelled or disqualified. 21.3.2, 21.3.3, D9

The Libero can be **declared** unable to play for any reason by the coach or, in the absence of a coach, by the assistant coach or by the game captain. 5.1.2.1,5.2.1

19.4.2 Team with one Libero:

19.4.2.1 When only one Libero is available for a team according to Rule 19.4.1, or the team has only one registered, and this Libero becomes or is declared unable to play, the coach (or game captain if no coach is present) may re-designate as Libero for the remainder of the match any other player (replacement player excepted) not on the court at the moment of the re-designation. 19.4,19.4.1

19.4.2.2 If the Acting Libero becomes unable to play, he/she may be replaced by the regular replacement player or immediately and directly to court by a re-designated Libero. However, a Libero who is the subject of a re-designation may not play for the remainder of the match.

对不合法的自由防守队员替换的处理等同于不合法的换人： 15.9

如果自由防守队员的不合法替换在下一比赛过程开始之前被发现并纠正，则该队应被判为延误比赛； 图 9

如果自由防守队员的不合法替换在发球击球之后被发现，则应判该队为不合法的换人。 15.9

19.4 指定新自由防守队员

19.4.1 当自由防守队员因受伤、生病、被判罚出场或被取消比赛资格等原因不能继续比赛时： 21.3.2, 21.3.3, 图 9

自由防守队员可以由教练员、助理教练员或场上队长（当教练员不在场时）以任何原因**宣布**不能继续比赛。 5.1.2.1,5.2.1

19.4.2 拥有 1 名自由防守队员的球队：

19.4.2.1 一支球队只有 1 名自由防守队员时，当出现规则 19.4.1 所述状况或虽然登记但宣布不能比赛时，教练员（教练员不在场时由场上队长）可以重新指定 1 名不在场上的队员（被自由防守队员替换的原场上队员除外）为新的自由防守队员； 19.4,19.4.1

19.4.2.2 如果场上自由防守队员宣布不能继续比赛时，可由原队员替换上场，或立即重新指定替换自由防守队员。但是，这名自由防守队员不能参与该场剩余比赛。

If the Libero is not on court when declared unable to play, he/she may also be the subject of a re-designation. The Libero declared unable to play may not play for the remainder of the match.

19.4.2.3 The coach, or assistant coach or game captain if no coach is present, contacts the second referee informing him/her about re-designation. 5.1.2.1,5.2.1

19.4.2.4 Should a re-designated Libero become or be declared unable to play, further re-designations are permitted. 19.4.1

19.4.2.5 If the coach requests the team captain to be re-designated as the new Libero, this will be permitted. 5.1.2, 19.4.1

19.4.2.6 In the case of a re-designated Libero, the number of the player redesignated as Libero must be recorded on the score sheet remarks section and on the Libero control sheet (or electronic score sheet if one is used.) 25.2.2.7, 28.2.2.1

19.4.3 Team with two Liberos

19.4.3.1 Where a team has registered on the score sheet two Liberos, but one becomes unable to play the team has the right to play with only one Libero. 4.1.1, 19.1.1

No re-designation will be allowed, however, unless the remaining Libero is unable to continue playing for the match. 19.4

19.5 SUMMARY

If the Libero is expelled or disqualified, he/she may be replaced immediately by the team's second Libero. Should the team have only one Libero, then it has the right to make a re-designation. 19.4, 21.3.2, 21.3.3

自由防守队员不在场上但宣布不能比赛时，也可重新指定自由防守队员。经宣布不能比赛的原自由防守队员不能参与该场后续的比赛；

19.4.2.3 教练员（教练员不在场时由助理教练员或场上队长）联系第 2 裁判员进行重新指定； 5.1.2.1,5.2.1

19.4.2.4 如果自由防守队员宣布不能继续比赛，重新指定不受次数限制； 19.4.1

19.4.2.5 如果教练员指定队长为新的自由防守队员是被允许的。 5.1.2, 19.4.1

19.4.2.6 新指定的自由防守队员应在记录表的备注栏里做记录，随后的替换在自由防守队员管理表（或电子记录表）上做记录。 25.2.2.7, 28.2.2.1

19.4.3 拥有两名自由防守队员的球队：

19.4.3.1 一支球队在记录表上登记了 2 名自由防守队员，当其中 1 名自由防守队员不能继续比赛时，该队有权只使用 1 名自由防守队员比赛； 4.1.1, 19.1.1

该队不得再指定新的自由防守队员，除非另一名自由防守队员也不能继续比赛。 19.4

19.5 概要

如果自由防守队员被判罚出场或被取消比赛资格，他可以被第 2 自由防守队员替换。如果该队只有 1 名自由防守队员，则有权指定新的自由防守队员。 19.4, 21.3.2, 21.3.3

CHAPTER 7

PARTICIPANTS' CONDUCT

See Rules

20 REQUIREMENTS OF CONDUCT

20.1 SPORTSMANLIKE CONDUCT

20.1.1 Participants must know the "Official Volleyball Rules" and abide by them.

20.1.2 Participants must accept referees' decisions with sportsmanlike conduct, without disputing them.

In case of doubt, clarification may be requested only through the game captain. 5.1.2.1

20.1.3 Participants must refrain from actions or attitudes aimed at influencing the decisions of the referees or covering up faults committed by their team.

20.2 FAIR PLAY

20.2.1 Participants must behave respectfully and courteously in the spirit of FAIR PLAY, not only towards the referees, but also towards other officials, the opponent, team-mates and spectators.

20.2.2 Communication between team members during the match is permitted. 5.2.3.4

第七节
参赛者的行为

参照规则

20　行为要求

20.1　体育道德

20.1.1　参赛者必须了解并遵守官方发布的排球竞赛规则。

20.1.2　参赛者必须以良好的体育道德行为服从裁判员的裁定，不允许进行争辩。

如有疑问，可以并只能通过场上队长提请解释。　5.1.2.1

20.1.3　参赛者不得有任何以影响裁判员判断或掩盖本队犯规为目的的动作或行为或态度。

20.2　公正竞赛

20.2.1　参赛者的行为必须符合“公正竞赛”的精神，这不仅指对裁判员，也包括对其他工作人员、对手、队友以及观众都要尊重、有礼貌。

20.2.2　比赛中，本队成员之间的交流是被允许的。　5.2.3.4

21 MISCONDUCT AND ITS SANCTIONS

21.1 MINOR MISCONDUCT

Minor misconduct offences are not subject to sanctions. It is the 1st referee' s duty to prevent the teams from approaching the sanctioning level. 5.1.2, 21.3

This is done in two stages: D9, D11 (6a)

Stage 1: by issuing a verbal warning through the game captain;

Stage 2: by use of a YELLOW CARD to the team member(s) concerned. This formal warning is not in itself a sanction but a symbol that the team member (and by extension the team) has reached the sanctioning level for the match. It is recorded in the score sheet but has no immediate consequences.

21.2 MISCONDUCT LEADING TO SANCTIONS

Incorrect conduct by a team member towards officials, opponents, team-mates or spectators is classified in three categories according to the seriousness of the offence. 4.1.1

21.2.1 Rude conduct: action contrary to good manners or moral principles.

21.2.2 Offensive conduct: defamatory or insulting words or gestures or any action expressing contempt.

21.2.3 Aggression: actual physical attack or aggressive or threatening behaviour.

21 不良行为及其处罚

21.1 轻微的不良行为

对轻微的不良行为不进行处罚，但第1裁判员有责任防止球队出现接近被处罚程度的行为。 5.1.2, 21.3

这里分两个步骤完成： 图9, 图11 (6a)

步骤1：通过场上队长进行口头警告；

步骤2：向相关球队的成员出示黄牌，虽然没有处罚，但要登记在记录表上，警告该队其行为已接近被处罚的程度。

21.2 给予处罚的不良行为

球队的成员对裁判员、对手、队友或观众存在不良行为时，按严重程度分为3类。 4.1.1

21.2.1 粗鲁行为：违背道德准则和文明举止的行为。

21.2.2 冒犯行为：诽谤或侮辱性的言语、形态以及任何轻蔑的表示。

21.2.3 侵犯行为：人身攻击、侵犯或威吓行为。

21.3 SANCTION SCALE

D9

According to the judgment of the 1st referee and depending on the seriousness of the offence, the sanctions to be applied and recorded on the score sheet are: **Penalty, Expulsion or Disqualification**. 21.2, 25.2.2.6

21.3.1 Penalty D11 (6b)

The first rude conduct in the match by any team member is penalized with a point and service to the opponent. 4.1.1, 21.2.1

21.3.2 Expulsion D11 (7)

21.3.2.1 A team member who is sanctioned by expulsion must be substituted legally/exceptionally and immediately if on court, shall not participate for the rest of the set, and must go to the team's dressing room until the completion of the ongoing set with no other consequences. 4.1.1, 5.2.1, 5.3.2, D1a, D1b

An expelled coach loses his/her right to intervene in the set and must go to the team's dressing room until the completion of the ongoing set. 5.2.3.3

21.3.2.2 The first offensive conduct by a team member is sanctioned by expulsion with no other consequences. 4.1.1, 21.2.2

21.3.2.3 The second rude conduct in the same match by the same team member is sanctioned by expulsion with no other consequences. 4.1.1, 21.2.1

21.3.3 Disqualification D11 (8)

21.3.3.1 A team member who is sanctioned by disqualification must be substituted legally/exceptionally and immediately if on court and must go to the team's dressing room for the rest of the match with no other consequences. 4.1.1, D1a

21.3　处罚等级

图 9

第 1 裁判员根据不良行为的程度，分别给予**判罚、判罚出场或取消比赛资格**的处罚，并登记在记录表上。 21.2, 25.2.2.6

21.3.1　判罚　图 11 (6b)

用于全场比赛中任何成员的第 1 次粗鲁行为，判对方得 1 分并发球。 4.1.1, 21.2.1

21.3.2　判罚出场　图 11 (7)

21.3.2.1　球队任何成员被判罚出场后不得继续参加该局剩余比赛，同时须到球队更衣室直至该局比赛结束，无其他判处。 4.1.1, 5.2.1, 5.3.2, 图 1a, 图 1b

教练员被判罚出场后失去其在本局指导比赛的权利，同时须到球队更衣室直至该局比赛结束。 5.2.3.3

21.3.2.2　球队任何成员第 1 次出现冒犯行为时，判罚其出场，无其他判处。 4.1.1, 21.2.2

21.3.2.3　同一成员在一场比赛中出现第 2 次粗鲁行为时，判罚其出场，无其他判处。 4.1.1, 21.2.1

21.3.3　取消比赛资格　图 11 (8)

21.3.3.1　球队任何成员被取消比赛资格后必须立刻进行合法替换或特殊替换（如他在场上），同时须到球队更衣室直至本场比赛结束，无其他判处。 4.1.1, 图 1a

21.3.3.2 The first physical attack or implied or threatened aggression is sanctioned by disqualification with no other consequences. 21.2.3

21.3.3.3 The second offensive conduct in the same match by the same team member is sanctioned by disqualification with no other consequences. 4.1.1, 21.2.2

21.3.3.4 The third rude conduct in the same match by the same team member is sanctioned by disqualification with no other consequences. 4.1.1, 21.2.1

21.4 APPLICATION OF MISCONDUCT SANCTIONS

21.4.1 All misconduct sanctions are individual sanctions, remain in force for the entire match and are recorded on the score sheet. 21.3, 25.2.2.6

21.4.2 The repetition of misconduct by the same team member in the same match is sanctioned progressively (the team member receives a heavier sanction for each successive offence). 4.1.1, 21.2, 21.3, D9

21.4.3 Expulsion or disqualification due to offensive conduct or aggression does not require a previous sanction. 21.2, 21.3

21.5 MISCONDUCT BEFORE AND BETWEEN SETS

Any misconduct occurring before or between sets is sanctioned according to Rule 21.3 and sanctions apply in the following set. 18.1, 21.2, 21.3

21.6 SUMMARY OF MISCONDUCT AND CARDS USED

D11 (6a, 6b, 7, 8)
21.1

Warning: no sanction

– Stage 1: verbal warning

21.3.3.2 球队任何成员第 1 次出现侵犯行为时，取消其比赛资格，无其他判处。 21.2.3

21.3.3.3 同一成员在一场比赛中出现第 2 次冒犯行为时，取消其比赛资格，无其他判处。 4.1.1, 21.2.2

21.3.3.4 同一成员在一场比赛中出现第 3 次粗鲁行为时，取消其比赛资格，无其他判处。 4.1.1, 21.2.1

21.4 处罚的实施

21.4.1 不良行为的判处是针对个人的，且对全场比赛有效，并应记录在记录表上。 21.3, 25.2.2.6

21.4.2 同一成员在同一场比赛中重犯不良行为时，按处罚等级加一级处罚（该成员接受的处罚要重于前一次）。 4.1.1, 21.2, 21.3, 图 9

21.4.3 对冒犯行为或侵犯行为予以判罚出场或取消比赛资格时，无须有先一次的判处。 21.2, 21.3

21.5 局前与局间的不良行为

任何局前与局间的不良行为，都应按规则 21.3 进行处置，并在下一局中判罚。 18.1, 21.2, 21.3

21.6 不良行为的种类与红黄牌的使用

图11 (6a, 6b, 7, 8) 21.1

警告：没有处罚

— 步骤 1：口头警告

– Stage 2: symbol Yellow card

Penalty: sanction – symbol Red card 21.3.1

Expulsion: sanction – symbol Red + Yellow cards jointly 21.3.2

Disqualification: sanction – symbol Red + Yellow card separately 21.3.3

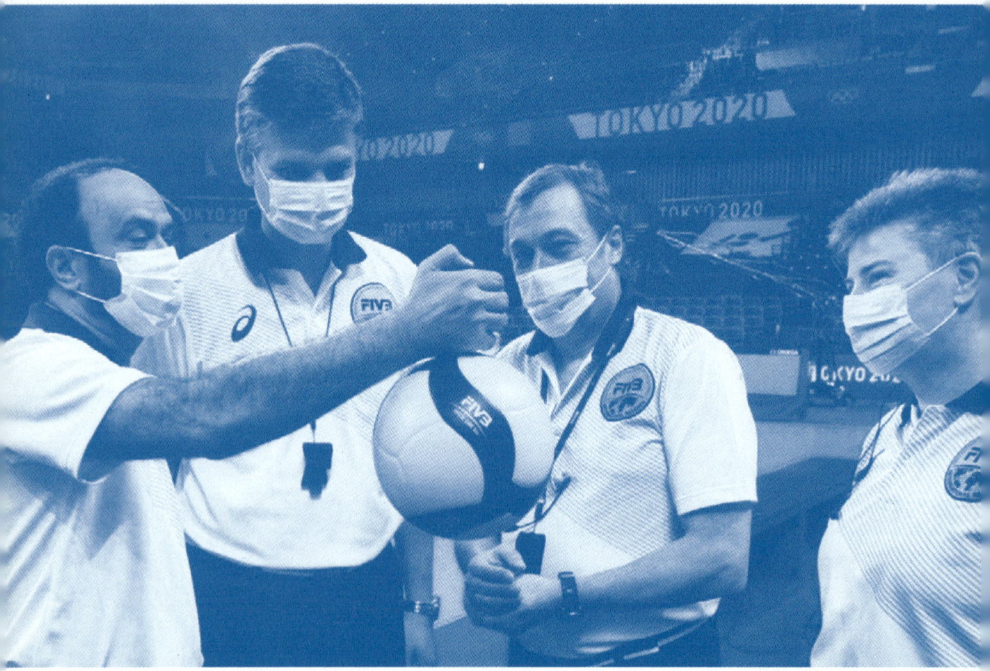

— 步骤 2：出示黄牌

判罚：出示红牌 21.3.1

判罚出场：单手出示红牌 + 黄牌 21.3.2

取消比赛资格：双手分别出示红牌 + 黄牌 21.3.3

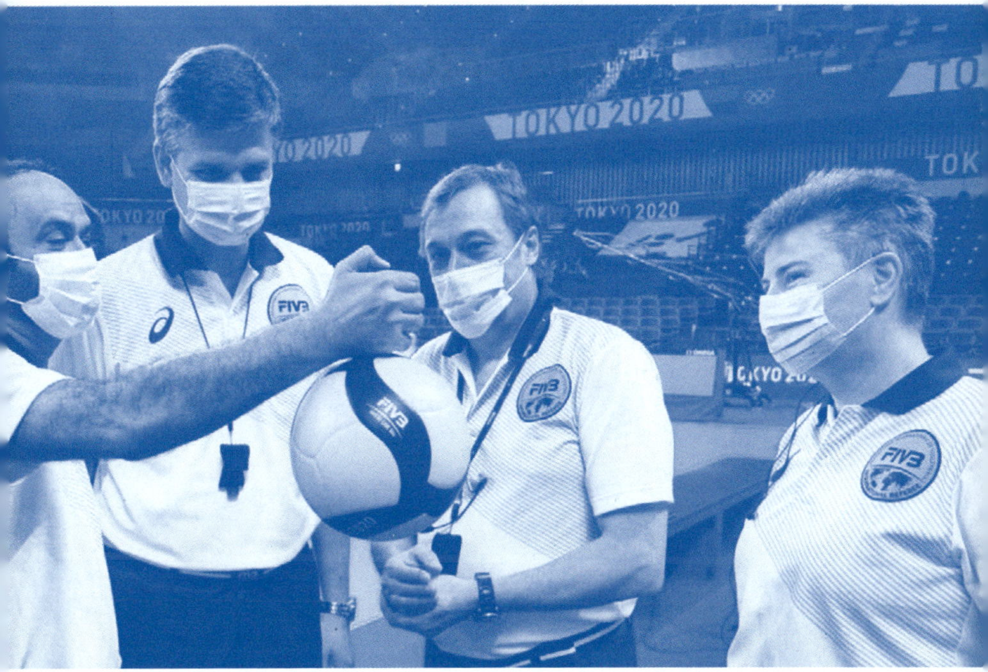

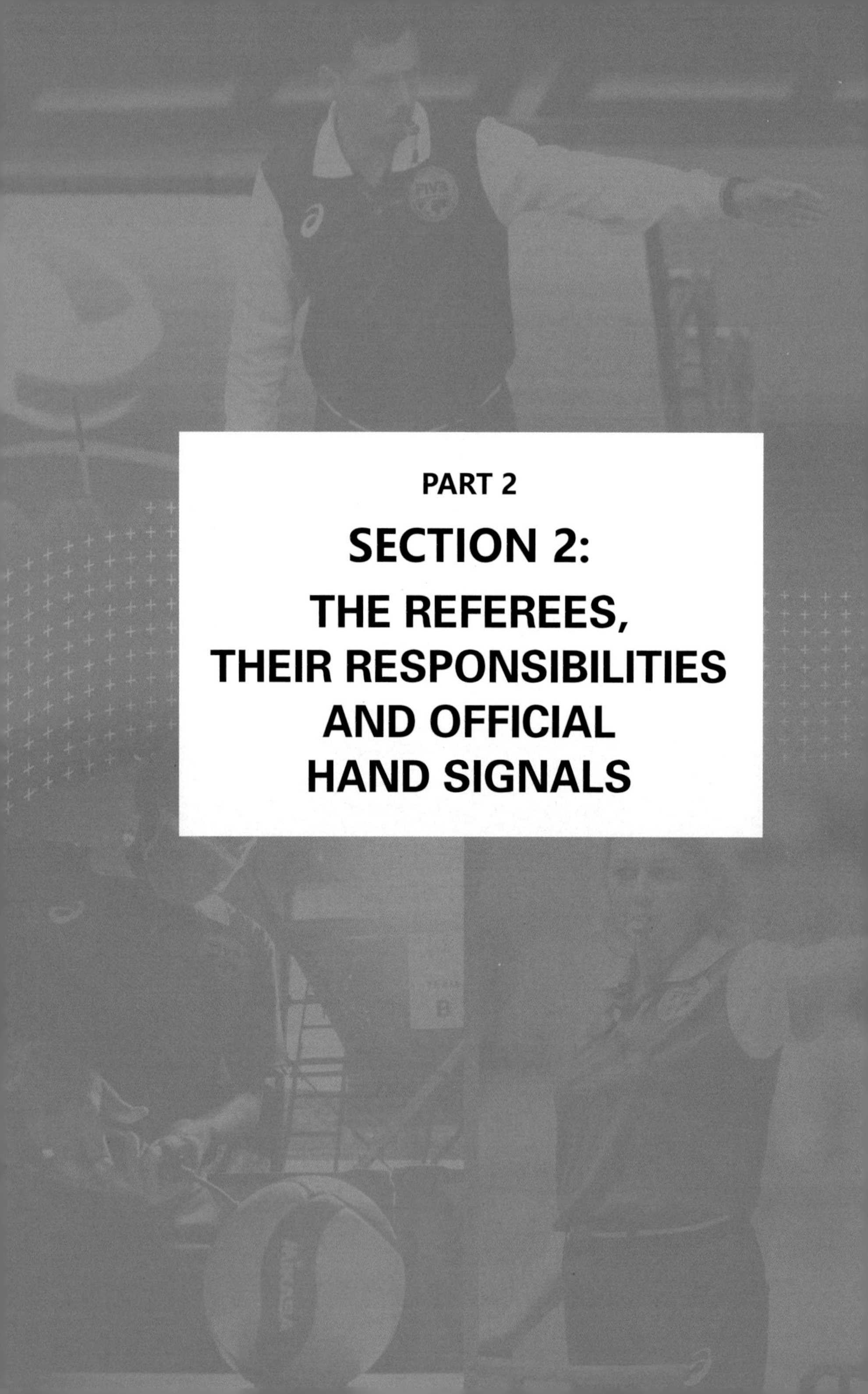

PART 2

SECTION 2:

THE REFEREES, THEIR RESPONSIBILITIES AND OFFICIAL HAND SIGNALS

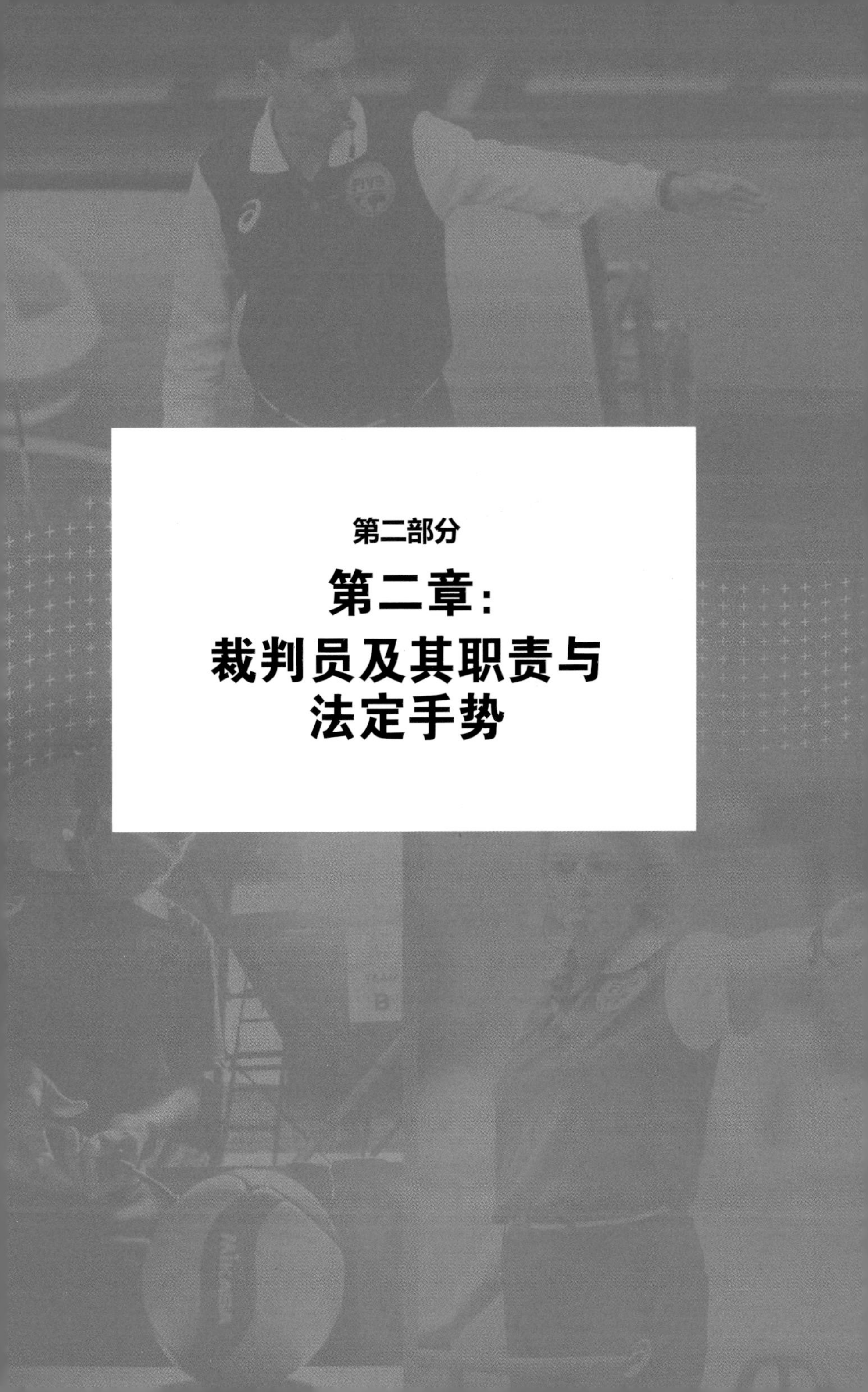

第二部分

第二章：

裁判员及其职责与法定手势

CHAPTER 8

REFEREES

See Rules

22 REFEREEING TEAM AND PROCEDURES

22.1 COMPOSITION

The refereeing team for a match is composed of the following officials:

– the 1st referee, 23
– the 2nd referee, 24
– the Challenge referee, 25
– the reserve referee, 26
– the scorer, 27, 28
– four (two) line judges. 29

Their location is shown in Diagram 10.

For FIVB, World and Official Competitions a Challenge referee (if VCS is in use), a Reserve referee and an Assistant scorer are compulsory. 25, 26, 28

22.2 PROCEDURES

22.2.1 Only the 1st and 2nd referees may blow a whistle during the match:

22.2.1.1 the 1st referee gives the signal for the service that begins the rally; 6.1.3, 12.3, D11 (1)

第八节
裁判员

参照规则

22　裁判团队与工作程序

22.1　组成

一场比赛的裁判团队由以下人员组成：

——第 1 裁判员； 23
——第 2 裁判员； 24
——挑战裁判员； 25
——替补裁判员； 26
——记录员； 27, 28
——4 名（2 名）司线员。 29

他们的位置如图 10 所示。

国际排联（FIVB）比赛、世界性比赛和正式比赛应设一名挑战裁判员（如使用鹰眼设备）、一名替补裁判员和一名辅助记录员。 25, 26, 28

22.2　工作程序

22.2.1　比赛进行中只有第 1 裁判员和第 2 裁判员可以鸣哨：

22.2.1.1　第 1 裁判员鸣哨发球开始比赛； 6.1.3, 12.3, 图 11 (1)

22.2.1.2 the 1st or 2nd referee signals the end of the rally, provided that they are sure that a fault has been committed and they have identified its nature. 5.1.2, 8.2

22.2.2 They may blow the whistle when the ball is out of play to indicate that they authorize or reject a team request. 22.2.1.2, 30.1

22.2.3 Immediately after the referee' s whistle to signal the completion of the rally, they have to indicate with the official hand signals:

22.2.3.1 if the fault is whistled by the 1st referee, he/she will indicate in order:

a) the team to serve, 12.2.2, D11 (2)
b) the nature of the fault,
c) the player(s) at fault (if necessary).

22.2.3.2 If the fault is whistled by the 2nd referee, he/she will indicate:

a) the nature of the fault,
b) the player at fault (if necessary),
c) the team to serve following the hand signal of the 1st referee. 12.2.2

In this case, the 1st referee does not show **either** the nature of the fault or the player at fault, but only the team to serve. D11 (2)

22.2.3.3 In the case of an attack hit fault or blocking fault by back row or Libero players, both referees indicate according to 22.2.3.1 and 22.2.3.2 above. 12.2.2, 13.3.3, 13.3.5, 19.3.1.2, 23.3.2.3d, e, D11 (21)

22.2.3.4 In the case of a double fault both referees indicate in order:

a) the nature of the fault, 17.3, D11 (23)

22.2.1.2 第 1 裁判员和第 2 裁判员确认犯规发生并判明其性质，鸣哨中止比赛。 5.1.2, 8.2

22.2.2 在比赛中断期间，他们可以鸣哨表示同意或拒绝一支球队的请求。 22.2.1.2, 30.1

22.2.3 裁判员鸣哨中止比赛后，应立即以法定手势表明：

22.2.3.1 如果是第 1 裁判员鸣哨中止比赛，他应指出：

a) 发球的队； 12.2.2, 图 11 (2)
b) 犯规的性质；
c) 犯规的队员（必要时）。

22.2.3.2 如果是第 2 裁判员鸣哨中止比赛，他应指出：

a) 犯规的性质；
b) 犯规的队员（必要时）；
c) 跟随第 1 裁判员指出发球的队。 12.2.2

第 1 裁判员不用同时再出示犯规性质和犯规队员的手势，只指出发球队。 图 11 (2)

22.2.3.3 如果后排队员或自由防守队员进攻性击球犯规，则两名裁判员都应根据规则 22.2.3.1 和 22.2.3.2 做出手势。 12.2.2, 13.3.3, 13.3.5, 19.3.1.2, 23.3.2.3d, e, 图 11 (21)

22.2.3.4 如果是双方犯规，他们都要按顺序指出：

a) 犯规的性质； 17.3, 图 11 (23)

b) the players at fault (if necessary),

The team to serve next is then indicated by the 1st referee. 12.2.2, D11 (2)

23 1st REFEREE

23.1 LOCATION

The 1st referee carries out his/her functions standing on a referee's stand located at one end of the net on the opposite side to the scorer. His/her view must be approximately 50 cm above the net. D1a, D1b, D10

23.2 AUTHORITY

23.2.1 The 1st referee directs the match from the start until the end. He/she has authority over all members of the refereeing team and the members of the teams. 4.1.1, 6.3

During the match his/her decisions are final. He/she is authorized to overrule the decisions of other members of the refereeing team, if it is noticed that they are mistaken.

He/she may even replace a member of the refereeing team who is not performing his/her functions properly.

23.2.2 He/she also controls the work of the ball retrievers, and quick moppers. 3.3

23.2.3 He/she has the power to decide any matters involving the game, including those not provided for in the rules.

23.2.4 He/she shall not permit any discussion about his/her decisions. 20.1.2

b) 犯规的队员（必要时）。

应发球的球队由第 1 裁判员指出。 12.2.2, 图 11 (2)

23　第 1 裁判员

23.1　位置

第 1 裁判员坐或站在记录台对面的球网一端的裁判台上执行其职责。他的视线水平位置应高出球网上沿约 50 厘米。 图 1a, 图 1b, 图 10

23.2　权力

23.2.1　第 1 裁判员自始至终领导该场比赛，对所有裁判员和球队成员行使权力。 4.1.1, 6.3

比赛中，他的判定是最终判定。如果发现其他裁判员的判断有误，第 1 裁判员有权改判。

他甚至可以撤换一名不称职的裁判员。

23.2.2　他同样掌管捡球员和快擦员的工作。 3.3

23.2.3　他有权决定涉及比赛的问题，包括规则中没有规定的问题。

23.2.4　他不允许对其判定进行任何讨论。 20.1.2

However, at the request of the game captain, the 1st referee will give an explanation on the application or interpretation of the rules upon which he/she has based the decision. 5.1.2.1

If the game captain does not agree with this explanation and chooses to protest against such decision, he/she must immediately reserve the right to file and record this protest at the conclusion of the match. The 1st referee must authorize this right of the game captain. 5.1.2.1, 5.1.3.2, 25.2.3.2

23.2.5 The 1st referee is responsible for determining before and during the match whether the playing area equipment and the conditions meet playing requirements. Chapter 1, 23.3.1.1

23.3 RESPONSIBILITIES

23.3.1 Prior to the match, the 1st referee:

23.3.1.1 inspects the conditions of the playing area, the balls and other equipment; Chapter 1, 23.2.5

23.3.1.2 performs the toss with the team captains; 7.1

23.3.1.3 controls the teams' warming-up. 7.2

23.3.2 During the match, he/she is authorized:

23.3.2.1 to issue warnings to the teams; 21.1

23.3.2.2 to sanction misconduct and delays; 16.2, 21.2, D9,D11 (6a, 6b, 7, 8, 25)

23.3.2.3 to decide upon:

a) the faults of the server and of the positions of the serving team, including the screen; 7.5, 12.4, 12.5, 12.7.1, D4, D6,D11 (12, 13, 22)

但当场上队长提出请求时，他应对该判定所依据的规则和规则的执行给予解释。 5.1.2.1

如果场上队长表示不同意解释，并立即声明保留比赛结束后将抗议写在记录表上的要求时，第1裁判员必须准许。 5.1.2.1, 5.1.3.2, 25.2.3.2

23.2.5　比赛前和比赛中，第1裁判员负责决定赛场条件是否符合比赛要求。 第一节，23.3.1.1

23.3　职责

23.3.1　比赛前，第1裁判员：

23.3.1.1　检查场地、比赛用球和器材； 第一节，23.2.5

23.3.1.2　主持双方队长的抽签； 7.1

23.3.1.3　掌握两队的准备活动。 7.2

23.3.2　比赛中，第1裁判员有权：

23.3.2.1　向球队提出警告； 21.1

23.3.2.2　对不良行为和延误比赛进行处置。 16.2, 21.2, 图9, 图11 (6a, 6b, 7, 8, 25)

23.3.2.3　判定：

a) 发球犯规和发球队位置错误，包括发球掩护； 7.5, 12.4, 12.5, 12.7.1，图4, 图6, 图11 (12, 13, 22)

b) the faults in playing the ball; 9.3,D11 (16, 17, 18)

c) the faults above the net, and the faulty contact of the player with the net, primarily (but not exclusively) on the attacker' s side; 11.3.1,11.4.1, 11.4.4, D11 (20)

d) the attack hit faults of the Libero and back-row players; 13.3.3, 13.3.5, 24.3.2.4, D8, D11 (21)

e) the completed attack hits made by a player on a ball above net height coming from an overhand pass with fingers by the Libero in his/her front zone; 1.4.1, 13.3.6, 24.3.2.4, D11 (21)

f) the ball crossing completely the lower space under the net; 8.4.5, 24.3.2.7, D5a, D11 (22)

g) the completed block by back row players or the attempted block by the Libero. 14.6.2, 14.6.6, D11 (12)

h) the ball that crosses the net totally or partly outside of the crossing space to the opponent' s court or contacts the antenna on his/her side of the playing court. D11 (15)

i) the served ball and the 3rd hit passing over or outside the antenna on his/ her side of the court. D11 (15)

23.3.3 At the end of the match, he/she checks the score sheet and signs it. 24.3.3, 25.2.3.3

24 2nd REFEREE

24.1 LOCATION

The 2nd referee performs his/her functions standing outside the playing court near the post, on the opposite side of and facing the 1st referee. D1a, D1b, D10

b) 比赛中击球的犯规； 9.3, 图 11 (16, 17, 18)

c) 主要（但不限于）在进攻一方的高于球网的犯规和队员触网的犯规； 11.3.1,11.4.1, 11.4.4, 图 11 (20)

d) 自由防守队员和后排队员的进攻性击球犯规； 13.3.3, 13.3.5, 24.3.2.4, 图 8, 图 11 (21)

e) 自由防守队员在前场区及延长区进行上手传球后，本方队员在球高于球网处完成进攻性击球的犯规行为； 1.4.1, 13.3.6, 24.3.2.4, 图 11 (21)

f) 球的整体从球网下方空间穿越； 8.4.5, 24.3.2.7, 图 5a, 图 11 (22)

g) 后排队员完成拦网或自由防守队员试图拦网； 14.6.2, 14.6.6, 图 11 (12)

h) 球的整体或部分从他一侧的过网区以外进入对方场地或触及标志杆； 图 11 (15)

i) 发球或第三次击球时，球从他一侧的标志杆上方或外侧通过。 图 11 (15)

23.3.3　比赛结束后，检查记录表并签字。 24.3.3, 25.2.3.3

24　第 2 裁判员

24.1　位置

第 2 裁判员站在第 1 裁判员对面、比赛场区外的网柱附近，面对第 1 裁判员执行其职责。 图 1a, 图 1b, 图 10

24.2 AUTHORITY

24.2.1 The 2nd referee is the assistant of the 1st referee, but has also his/her own range of jurisdiction. 24.3

Should the 1st referee become unable to continue his/her work, the 2nd referee may replace him/her.

24.2.2 He/she may, without whistling, also signal faults outside his/her range of jurisdiction, but may not insist on them to the 1st referee. 24.3

24.2.3 He/she controls the work of the scorer(s). 25.2, 28.2

24.2.4 He/she supervises the team members on the team bench and reports their misconduct to the 1st referee. 4.2.1

24.2.5 He/she controls the players in the warm-up areas. 4.2.3

24.2.6 He/she authorizes the regular game interruptions, controls their duration and rejects improper requests. 15, 15.11, 25.2.2.3

24.2.7 He/she controls the number of time-outs and substitutions used by each team and reports the 2nd time-out and 5th and 6th substitutions to the 1st referee and the coach concerned. 15.1, 25.2.2.3

24.2.8 In the case of an injury of a player, he/she authorizes an exceptional substitution or grants a 3-minute recovery time. 15.7, 17.1.2

24.2.9 He/she checks the floor condition, mainly in the front zone. He/she also checks, during the match, that the balls still fulfil the regulations. 1.2.1, 3

24.2.10 **For FIVB, World and Official Competitions, the duty recorded under 24.2.5 is carried out by the Reserve Referee.** 26.2.6

24.2 权力

24.2.1	第 2 裁判员是第 1 裁判员的助手，但是也有自己的权限。 当第 1 裁判员不能继续工作时，第 2 裁判员可以代替其执行职责。	24.3
24.2.2	他可以用手势指出其权限以外的犯规，但不得鸣哨，也不得向第 1 裁判员坚持自己的判断。	24.3
24.2.3	他掌管记录员的工作。	25.2, 28.2
24.2.4	他监督坐在球队席上的球队成员，并将他们的不良行为报告给第 1 裁判员。	4.2.1
24.2.5	他掌管准备活动区域中的队员。	4.2.3
24.2.6	他允许合法比赛间断的请求，掌握间断时间和拒绝不符合规定的请求。	15, 15.11, 25.2.2.3
24.2.7	他掌握各队暂停和换人的次数，并将第 2 次暂停和第 5、6 次换人告诉第 1 裁判员和有关教练员。	15.1, 25.2.2.3
24.2.8	发现队员受伤时，他可以允许特殊换人，或给予 3 分钟的恢复时间。	15.7, 17.1.2
24.2.9	他检查比赛场地的条件，主要是前场区。比赛中，他还要检查球是否符合比赛要求。	1.2.1, 3
24.2.10	**国际排联（FIVB）比赛、世界性比赛和正式比赛中，规则 24.2.5 表述的职责由替补裁判员执行。**	26.2.6

24.3 RESPONSIBILITIES

24.3.1 At the start of each set, at the change of courts in the deciding set and whenever necessary, the 2nd referee checks that the actual positions of the players on the court correspond to those on the line-up sheets. 5.2.3.1, 7.3.2, 7.3.5, 18.2.2

24.3.2 During the match, he/she decides, whistles and signals:

24.3.2.1 penetration into the opponent's court, and the space under the net; 1.3.3, 11.2, D5a, D11 (22)

24.3.2.2 positional faults of the receiving team; 7.5, D4, D11 (13)

24.3.2.3 the faulty contact of the player with the net primarily (but not exclusively) on the blocker's side and with the antenna on his/her side of the court; 11.3.1

24.3.2.4 the completed block by back row players or the attempted block by the Libero; or the attack hit fault by back row players or by the Libero; 13.3.3, 14.6.2, 14.6.6, 23.3.2.3d, e, g,D8, D11 (12, 21)

24.3.2.5 the contact of the ball with an outside object; 8.4.2, 8.4.3, D11 (15)

24.3.2.6 the contact of the ball with the floor when the 1st referee is not in position to see the contact; 8.3

24.3.2.7 the ball that crosses the net plane totally or partly outside of the crossing space to the opponent's court or contacts the antenna on his/ her side of the court; 8.4.3, 8.4.4, D5a, D11 (15)

24.3.2.8 the served ball and the 3rd hit passing over or outside the antenna on his/ her side of the court. D11 (15)

24.3.3 At the end of the match, he/she checks and signs the score sheet. 23.3.3, 25.2.3.3

24.3　职责

24.3.1	在每局开始和决胜局交换场区时，以及任何必要的时候，检查场上队员的实际位置是否与位置表相符。	5.2.3.1, 7.3.2, 7.3.5, 18.2.2
24.3.2	在比赛中，第 2 裁判员对以下犯规做出判断、鸣哨并做出手势：	
24.3.2.1	从球网下穿越进入对方场区和空间；	1.3.3, 11.2, 图 5a, 图 11 (22)
24.3.2.2	接发球队位置错误；	7.5, 图 4, 图 11 (13)
24.3.2.3	主要（但不限于）在拦网一方的队员触网犯规，以及触及第 2 裁判员一侧标志杆的犯规；	11.3.1
24.3.2.4	后排队员完成拦网和自由防守队员试图拦网的犯规，或后排队员和自由防守队员进攻性击球的犯规；	13.3.3, 14.6.2, 14.6.6, 23.3.2.3d, e, g, 图 8, 图 11 (12, 21)
24.3.2.5	球触及场外物体；	8.4.2, 8.4.3, 图 11 (15)
24.3.2.6	当球接触地面时，第 1 裁判员处于难以观察的位置；	8.3
24.3.2.7	球的整体或部分从过网区以外过网、飞入对方场区或触及他一侧的标志杆；	8.4.3, 8.4.4, 图 5a, 图 11 (15)
24.3.2.8	发球或第三次击球时，球从他一侧的标志杆上方或外侧通过。	图 11 (15)
24.3.3	比赛结束后，检查记录表并签字。	23.3.3, 25.2.3.3

25 CHALLENGE REFEREE

For FIVB, World and Official Competitions if the Video Challenge system is in use a Challenge referee is compulsory.

25.1 LOCATION

The Challenge referee carries out his/her functions in the challenge booth locating in a separate position determined by the FIVB Technical Delegate.

25.2 RESPONSIBILITIES

25.2.1 He/she supervises the challenge process and ensure, that it proceeds according to the challenge regulation in force.

25.2.2 The Challenge referee shall wear an official referee uniform while performing his/her functions.

25.2.3 After the challenge process he/she advises the 1st referee of the nature of the fault.

25.2.4 At the end of the match, he/she signs the score sheet.

26 RESERVE REFEREE

For FIVB, World and Official Competitions a Reserve referee is compulsory.

26.1 LOCATION

The Reserve referee carries out his/her functions locating in a separate position determined by the FIVB court layout.

25 挑战裁判员

国际排联（FIVB）比赛、世界性比赛和正式比赛如果使用鹰眼挑战系统（VCS），则必须设置一名挑战裁判员。

25.1 位置

挑战裁判员在一个独立的工作区内执行其职责，该位置由临场技术代表决定。

25.2 职责

25.2.1 他负责监督挑战过程并确保该过程遵照现行的挑战规则进行。

25.2.2 挑战裁判员在工作时应穿着正式裁判服。

25.2.3 经挑战过程认定后，他将犯规性质告知第1裁判员。

25.2.4 比赛结束后，他在记录表上签字。

26 替补裁判员

国际排联（FIVB）比赛、世界性比赛和正式比赛必须设置一名替补裁判员。

26.1 位置

替补裁判员根据国际排联（FIVB）场地布局图标定的工作位置执行其职责。

26.2 RESPONSIBILITIES

The Reserve referee is obliged to:

26.2.1 wear an official referee uniform while performing his/her functions;

26.2.2 replace the 2nd referee in case of absence or in case that he/she is unable to continue his/her work or in case that the 2nd referee became the 1st referee;

26.2.3 control the substitution paddles (if they are in use), before the match and between the sets;

26.2.4 check the operation of the bench tablets before and between the sets, if there is a problem;

26.2.5 assist the 2nd referee in keeping the free zone clear; 1.1

26.2.6 assist the 2nd referee in instructing the expelled/disqualified team-member to leave to the team's dressing room; 21.3.2.1, 21.3.3.1

26.2.7 control the substitute players in the warm-up area and on the bench; 1.4.5, 24.2.5, 24.2.10

26.2.8 bring to the 2nd referee four match balls, immediately after the presentation of the starting players and give the 2nd referee a match ball after he/she has finished checking the players' standing position; 24.3.1

26.2.9 assist the 1st referee with guiding the work of the moppers. 23.2.2

27 SCORER

27.1 LOCATION

The scorer performs his/her functions seated at the scorer's table on the opposite side of the court from and facing the 1st referee. D1a, D1b, D10

26.2　职责

替补裁判员的职责是：

26.2.1　在工作时应穿着正式裁判服；

26.2.2　当第 2 裁判员缺席或因故不能继续工作时，或者当第 2 裁判员变为第 1 裁判员后，接替第 2 裁判员的工作；

26.2.3　在赛前和局间管理换人牌（如果使用）；

26.2.4　如果球队席所配电子设备在每局前和每局进行中出现问题，应检查其运行情况；

26.2.5　协助第 2 裁判员维护无障碍区的整洁；　1.1

26.2.6　协助第 2 裁判员引导被判罚出场和被取消比赛资格的队员离开场地前往球队更衣室；　21.3.2.1, 21.3.3.1

26.2.7　管理在准备活动区及球队席的替补队员；　1.4.5, 24.2.5, 24.2.10

26.2.8　在比赛开始介绍首发队员后，立即向第 2 裁判员递交 4 个比赛用球，并在第 2 裁判员核对站位后再向其递交 1 个比赛用球；　24.3.1

26.2.9　协助第 1 裁判员指导擦地员的工作。　23.2.2

27　记录员

27.1　位置

记录员坐在第 1 裁判员对面的记录台处，面对第 1 裁判员执行其职责。　图 1a, 图 1b, 图 10

27.2 RESPONSIBILITIES

He/she fills in the score sheet according to the rules, co-operating with the 2nd referee.

He/she uses a buzzer or other sound device to notify irregularities or give signals to the referees on the basis of his/her responsibilities.

27.2.1 Prior to the match and set, the scorer:

27.2.1.1 registers the data of the match and teams, including the names and numbers of the Liberos, according to the procedures in force, and obtains the signatures of the captains and the coaches; 4.1, 5.1.1, 5.2.2, 7.3.2, 19.1.2, 19.4.2.6

27.2.1.2 records the starting line-up of each team from the line-up sheet (or checks the data submitted electronically). 5.2.3.1, 7.3.2

If he/she fails to receive the line-up sheets on time, he/she immediately notifies this fact to the 2nd referee. 5.2.3.1

27.2.2 During the match, the scorer:

27.2.2.1 records the points scored; 6.1

27.2.2.2 controls the serving order of each team and indicates any error to the referees immediately after the service hit; 12.2

27.2.2.3 is empowered to acknowledge and announce requests for player substitutions by use of the buzzer, controlling their number, and records the substitutions and time-outs, informing the 2nd referee; 15.1, 15.4.1, 15.10.3.3, 24.2.6, 24.2.7

27.2.2.4 notifies the referees of a request for regular game interruption that is out of order; 15.11

27.2.2.5 announces to the referees the ends of the sets, and the scoring of the 8th point in the deciding set; 6.2, 15.4.1, 18.2.2

27.2　职责

根据规则与第 2 裁判员合作填写记录表。

基于自己的职责，他通过蜂鸣器或其他声响设备通知裁判员不符合规则的行为或发出信号。

27.2.1　在比赛前和每局前，记录员：

27.2.1.1 按照规定程序登记有关比赛和比赛队的情况，包括自由防守队员的姓名、号码，并获取双方队长和教练员的签字； 4.1, 5.1.1, 5.2.2, 7.3.2, 19.1.2, 19.4.2.6

27.2.1.2 根据位置表登记各队的首发阵容（或者检查电子系统提供的数据）。 5.2.3.1, 7.3.2

如果没有按时收到位置表，应立即通知第 2 裁判员。 5.2.3.1

27.2.2　在比赛中，记录员：

27.2.2.1 记录得分； 6.1

27.2.2.2 掌握各队的发球次序，发现发球次序错误时，应在发球击球后立即通知裁判员； 12.2

27.2.2.3 以蜂鸣器认可并宣告换人请求，掌握并登记暂停和换人次数和暂停，并通知第 2 裁判员； 15.1, 15.4.1, 15.10.3.3, 24.2.6, 24.2.7

27.2.2.4 对违背规则的正常比赛间断请求要通知裁判员； 15.11

27.2.2.5 每局结束及决胜局第 8 分时，向裁判员宣布； 6.2, 15.4.1, 18.2.2

27.2.2.6 records misconduct warnings, sanctions and improper requests; 15.11.3, 16.2, 21.3

27.2.2.7 records all other events as instructed by the 2nd referee, i.e. exceptional substitutions, recovery time, prolonged interruptions, external interference, re-designation, etc.; 15.7, 17.1.2, 17.2, 17.3, 19.4

27.2.2.8 controls the interval between sets. 18.1

27.2.3 At the end of the match, the scorer:

27.2.3.1 records the final result; 6.3

27.2.3.2 in the case of protest, with the previous authorization of the 1st referee, writes or permits the team/game captain to write on the score sheet a statement on the incident being protested; 5.1.2.1, 5.1.3.2, 23.2.4

27.2.3.3 signs the score sheet him/herself, before obtaining the signatures of the team captains and then the referees. 5.1.3.1, 23.3.3, 24.3.3

28 ASSISTANT SCORER

28.1 LOCATION

22.1, D1a, D1b, D10

The assistant scorer performs his/her functions seated beside the scorer at the scorer's table.

For FIVB, World and Official Competitions an assistant scorer is compulsory.

28.2 RESPONSIBILITIES

19.3

He/she records the replacements involving the Libero.

He/she assists with the administrative duties of the scorer's work.

27.2.2.6 记录警告、处罚的情况和不符合规定的请求； 15.11.3, 16.2, 21.3

27.2.2.7 在第 2 裁判员的指导下登记其他事件，如特殊换人、恢复时间、被拖延的间断、由外因造成的间断、重新指定，等等； 15.7, 17.1.2, 17.2, 17.3, 19.4

27.2.2.8 掌握局间休息。 18.1

27.2.3 在比赛结束后，记录员：

27.2.3.1 登记最终结果； 6.3

27.2.3.2 如果有提出抗议的情况并得到第 1 裁判员同意后，记录或允许队长将有关抗议的内容写在记录表上； 5.1.2.1, 5.1.3.2, 23.2.4

27.2.3.3 自己在记录表上签字后，取得双方队长和裁判员的签字。 5.1.3.1, 23.3.3, 24.3.3

28 辅助记录员

28.1 位置

22.1, 图 1a, 图 1b, 图 10

辅助记录员坐在记录员的身旁执行其职责。

国际排联（FIVB）比赛、世界性比赛和正式比赛必须设置一名辅助记录员。

28.2 职责

19.3

记录有关自由防守队员的替换。

协助记录员工作。

Should the scorer become unable to continue his/her work, the assistant scorer substitutes for the scorer.

28.2.1 Prior to the match and set, the assistant scorer:

28.2.1.1 prepares the Libero control sheet;

28.2.1.2 prepares the reserve score sheet.

28.2.2 During the match, the assistant scorer:

28.2.2.1 records the details of the Libero replacements/re-designations; 19.3.1.1, 19.4

28.2.2.2 notifies the referees of any fault of the Libero replacement, by using the buzzer; 19.3.2

28.2.2.3 operates the manual scoreboard on the scorer's table;

28.2.2.4 checks that the scoreboards agree; 27.2.2.1

28.2.2.5 if necessary, updates the reserve score sheet and gives it to the scorer. 27.2.1.1

28.2.3 At the end of the match, the assistant scorer:

28.2.3.1 signs the Libero control sheet and submits it for checking;

28.2.3.2 signs the score sheet.

For FIVB, World and Official Competitions which use an e-score sheet, the Assistant Scorer acts with the Scorer to announce the substitutions, to direct the 2nd Referee to the team requesting an interruption, and identify the Libero replacements.

记录员不能继续工作时，代替其工作。

28.2.1 比赛前和每局前，辅助记录员：

28.2.1.1 准备好自由防守队员管理表；

28.2.1.2 准备好备用记录表。

28.2.2 比赛中，辅助记录员：

28.2.2.1 详细记录自由防守队员正常的和特殊的替换； 19.3.1.1, 19.4

28.2.2.2 发现任何有关自由防守队员替换的犯规时，用蜂鸣器通知裁判员； 19.3.2

28.2.2.3 操作记录台上的手动记分牌；

28.2.2.4 监督记分牌的正确显示； 27.2.2.1

28.2.2.5 必要时填写好备用记录表的有关内容，交给记录员。 27.2.1.1

28.2.3 比赛结束后，辅助记录员：

28.2.3.1 在自由防守队员管理表上签字备查；

28.2.3.2 在记录表上签字。

国际排联（FIVB）比赛、世界性比赛和正式比赛使用电子记录表，辅助记录员协助记录员担任换人时的比分宣告、通知第2裁判员球队在比赛间断时的请求，以及鉴别自由防守队员的替换。

29 LINE JUDGES

29.1 LOCATION

D1a, D1b, D10

If only two line judges are used, they stand at the corners of the court closest to the right hand of each referee, diagonally at 1 to 2 m from the corner.

Each one of them controls both the end line and side line on his/her side.

For FIVB, World and Official Competitions if four line judges are used, they stand in the free zone at 1 to 3 m from each corner of the court, on the imaginary extension of the line that they control. D10

29.2 RESPONSIBILITIES

29.2.1 The line judges perform their functions by using flags (40 cm x 40 cm), to signal: D12

29.2.1.1 the ball "in" and "out" whenever the ball lands near their line(s); 8.3, 8.4, D12 (1, 2)

29.2.1.2 the touches of "out" balls by the team receiving the ball; 8.4, D12 (3)

29.2.1.3 the ball touching the antenna, the served ball and the third hit of the team crossing the net outside the crossing space, etc.; 8.4.3, 8.4.4, 10.1.1, D5a, D12 (4)

29.2.1.4 any player (except the server) stepping outside of his/her court at the moment of the service hit; 7.4, 12.4.3, D12 (4)

29.2.1.5 the foot faults of the server; 12.4.3

29.2.1.6 any contact with the top 80 cm of the antenna on their side of the court by any player during his/her action of playing the ball or interfering with the play; 11.3.1, 11.4.4, D3, D12 (4)

29　司线员

29.1　位置

如果只使用 2 名司线员，他们应分别站在第 1、2 裁判员右手一侧的场区角端、斜向位于场角 1 至 2 米处。 图 1a, 图 1b, 图 10

他们各自负责自己一侧的端线和边线。

国际排联（FIVB）比赛、世界性比赛和正式比赛中，如果使用 4 名司线员，他们应分别站在无障碍区内距每个场角 1 至 3 米处，即位于他们各自负责界线的假想延伸线上。 图 10

29.2　职责

29.2.1　司线员通过运用旗帜 (40 厘米 X40 厘米) 执行其职责，在下列情况下出示旗示： 图 12

29.2.1.1　当球落在他们所负责的界线附近时，示意球“界内”或“界外”； 8.3, 8.4, 图 12 (1, 2)

29.2.1.2　触及接球队员身体后出界的球，示意“触手出界”； 8.4, 图 12 (3)

29.2.1.3　示意球触及标志杆，示意发出的球和球队第三次击出的球从过网区外侧越过球网等； 8.4.3, 8.4.4, 10.1.1, 图 5a, 图 12 (4)

29.2.1.4　示意发球击球时队员的脚踏出场区 (发球队员除外)； 7.4, 12.4.3, 图 12 (4)

29.2.1.5　发球队员脚的犯规； 12.4.3

29.2.1.6　队员击球时或在干扰比赛的情况下，球触及他一侧标志杆高于球网上沿 80 厘米的部分； 11.3.1, 11.4.4, 图 3, 图 12 (4)

29.2.1.7 the ball crossing the net outside the crossing space into the opponent's court or touching the antenna on his/her side of the court. 10.1.1, D5a, D12 (4)

29.2.2 At the 1st referee's request, a line judge must repeat his/her signal.

30 OFFICIAL SIGNALS

30.1 REFEREES' HAND SIGNALS D11

The referees must indicate with the official hand signal the reason for their whistle (the nature of the fault whistled or the purpose of the interruption authorized). The signal has to be maintained for a moment and, if it is indicated with one hand, the hand corresponds to the side of the team which has made the fault or the request.

30.2 LINE JUDGES' FLAG SIGNALS D12

The line judges must indicate with the official flag signal the nature of the fault called, and maintain the signal for a moment.

29.2.1.7　球从标志杆外侧越过球网，并进入对方场区或触及他一侧的标志杆。　10.1.1, 图 5a, 图 12 (4)

29.2.2　在第 1 裁判员询问时，他必须重复旗示。

30　法定手势

30.1　裁判员的手势　图 11

裁判员必须以法定手势指出鸣哨的原因 (犯规的性质或准许的比赛间断的目的)。手势应有短时间的展示。如果是单手做手势，应使用与犯规队或请求队同侧的手表示。

30.2　司线员的旗示　图 12

司线员必须用法定的旗示表明犯规的性质，并有短时间的展示。

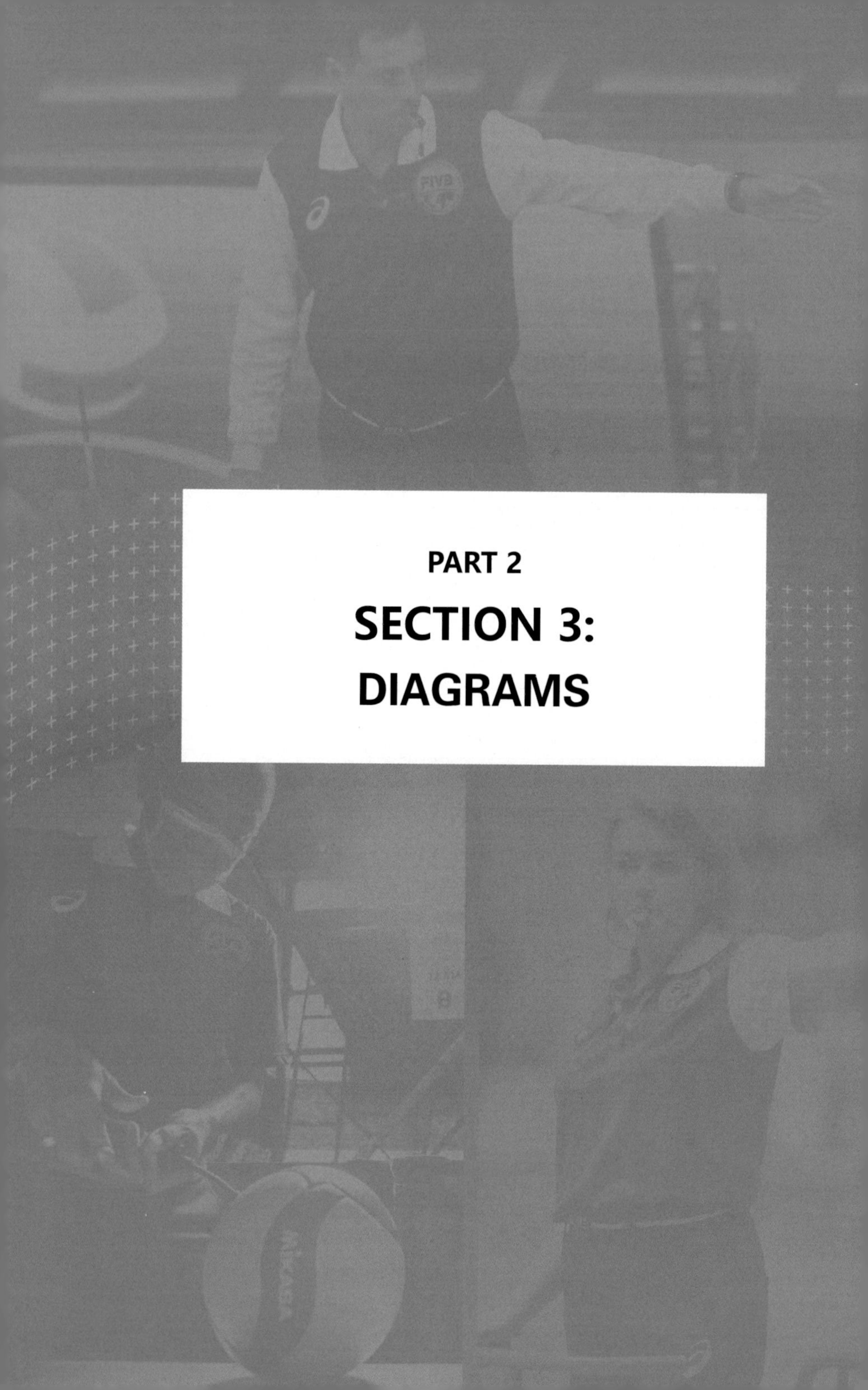

PART 2

SECTION 3: DIAGRAMS

第二部分

第三章：
图表

DIAGRAM 1a: COMPETITION / CONTROL AREA

Relevant Rules: 1, 1.4.5, 4.2.1, 4.2.3.1, 15.4.2, 21.3.2.1, 21.3.3.1, 27.1, 28.1

Values are valid for FIVB, World and Official Competitions

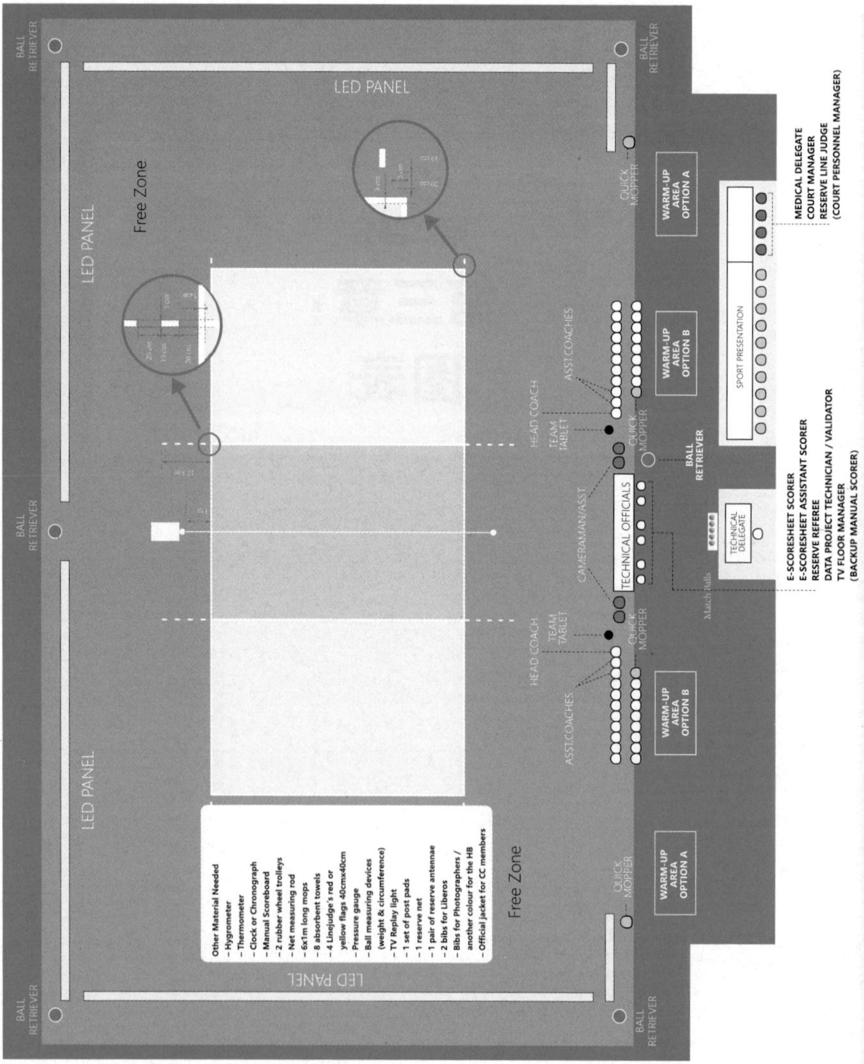

图 1a：竞赛控制区

相关规则： 1, 1.4.5, 4.2.1, 4.2.3.1, 15.4.2, 21.3.2.1, 21.3.3.1, 27.1, 28.1

国际排联（FIVB）比赛、世界性比赛和正式比赛使用的标准场地图

场地清晰大图

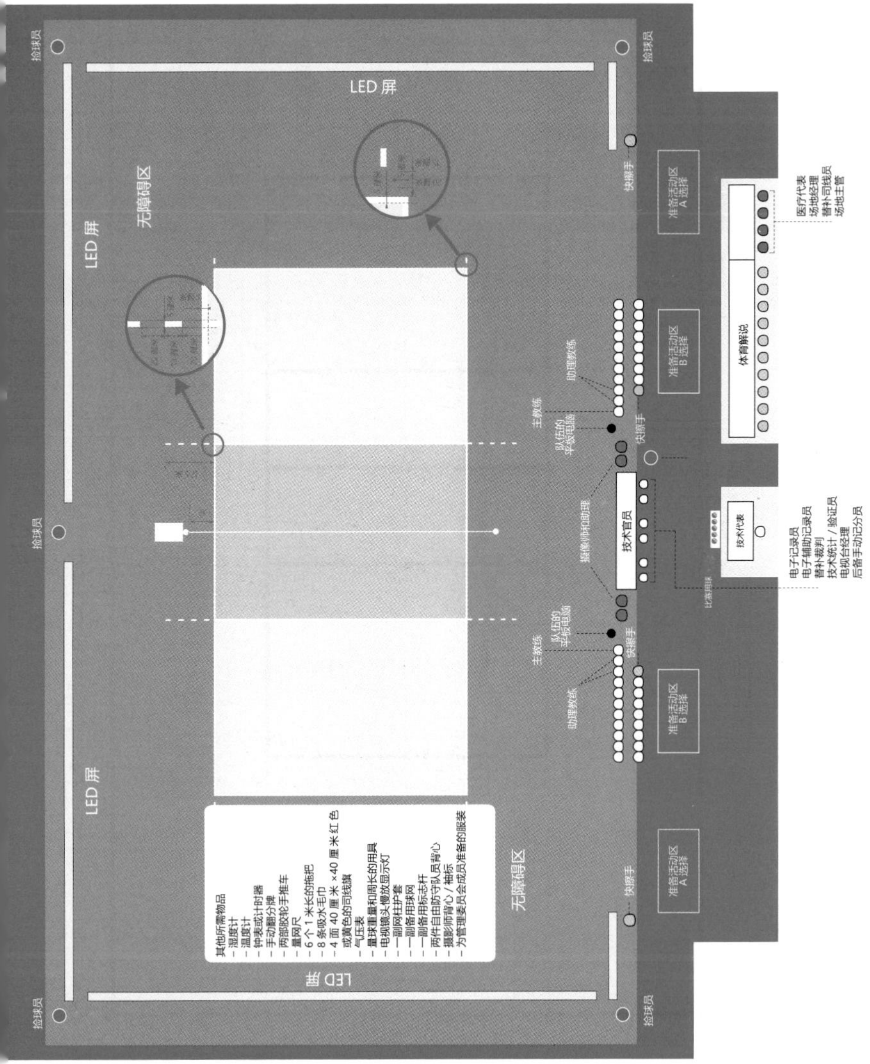

DIAGRAM 1b: THE PLAYING AREA

Relevant Rules: 1, 1.4, 1.4.2, 1.4.3, 1.4.4, 1.4.5, 4.2.1, 4.2.3.1, 15.10.1, 19.3.1.4, 19.3.2.7, 23.1, 24.1, 27.1, 28.1

Values are valid for FIVB, World and Official Competitions

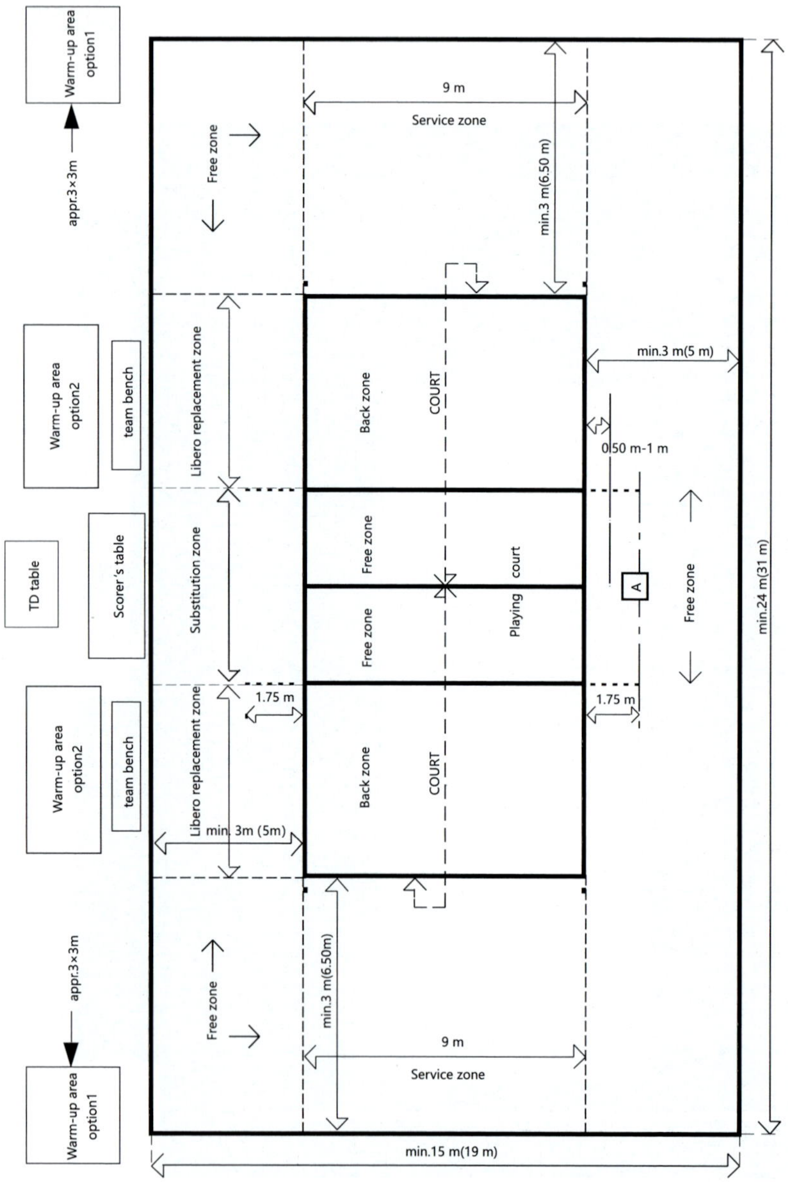

图 1b：比赛场地

相关规则： 1, 1.4, 1.4.2, 1.4.3, 1.4.4, 1.4.5, 4.2.1, 4.2.3.1, 15.10.1, 19.3.1.4, 19.3.2.7, 23.1, 24.1,27.1, 28.1

国际排联（FIVB）比赛、世界性比赛和正式比赛使用的标准场地图

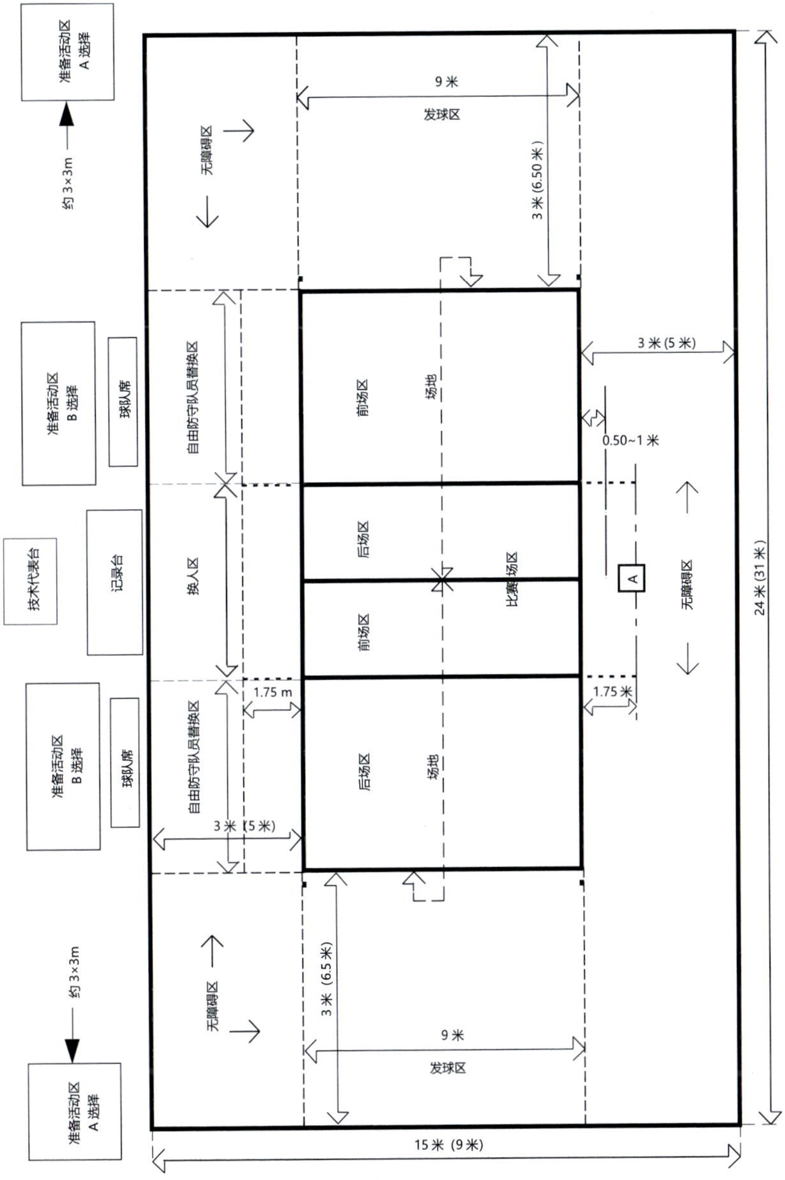

DIAGRAM 2: THE PLAYING COURT

Relevant Rules: 1.1, 1.3, 1.3.3, 1.3.4, 1.4.1

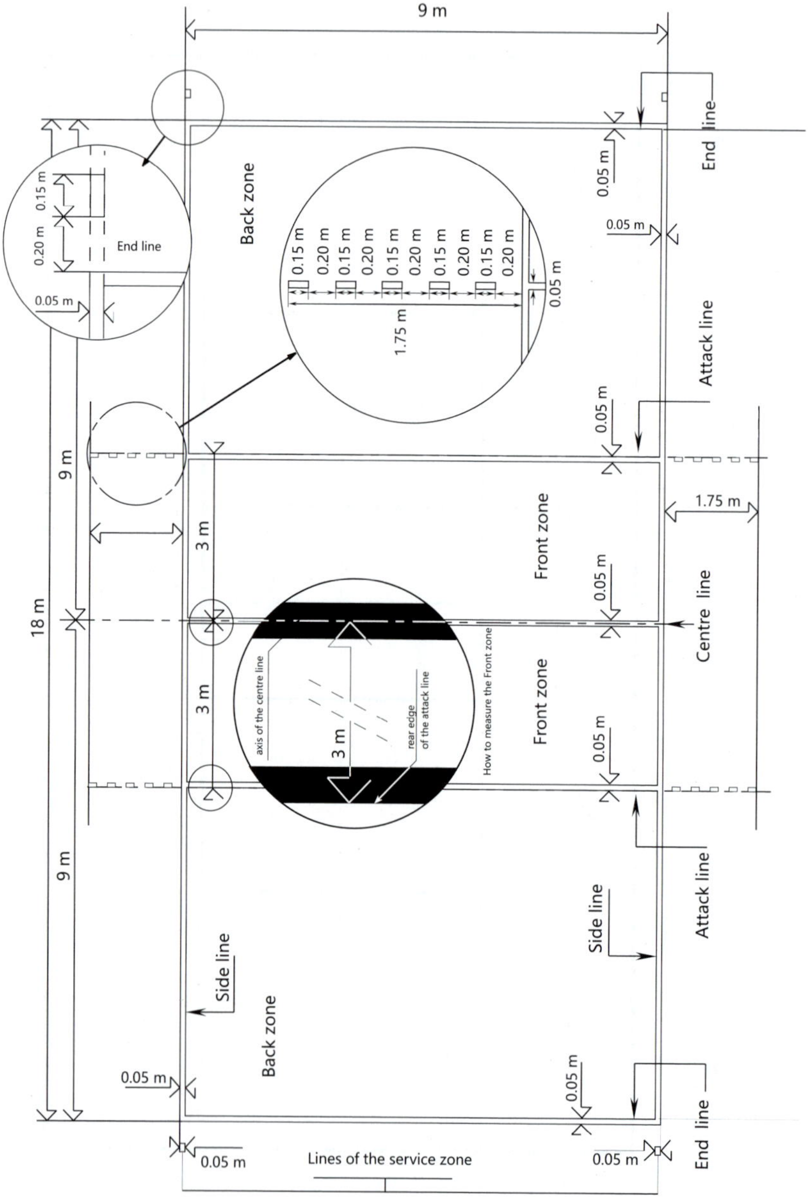

图 2：比赛场区

相关规则：1.1, 1.3, 1.3.3, 1.3.4, 1.4.1

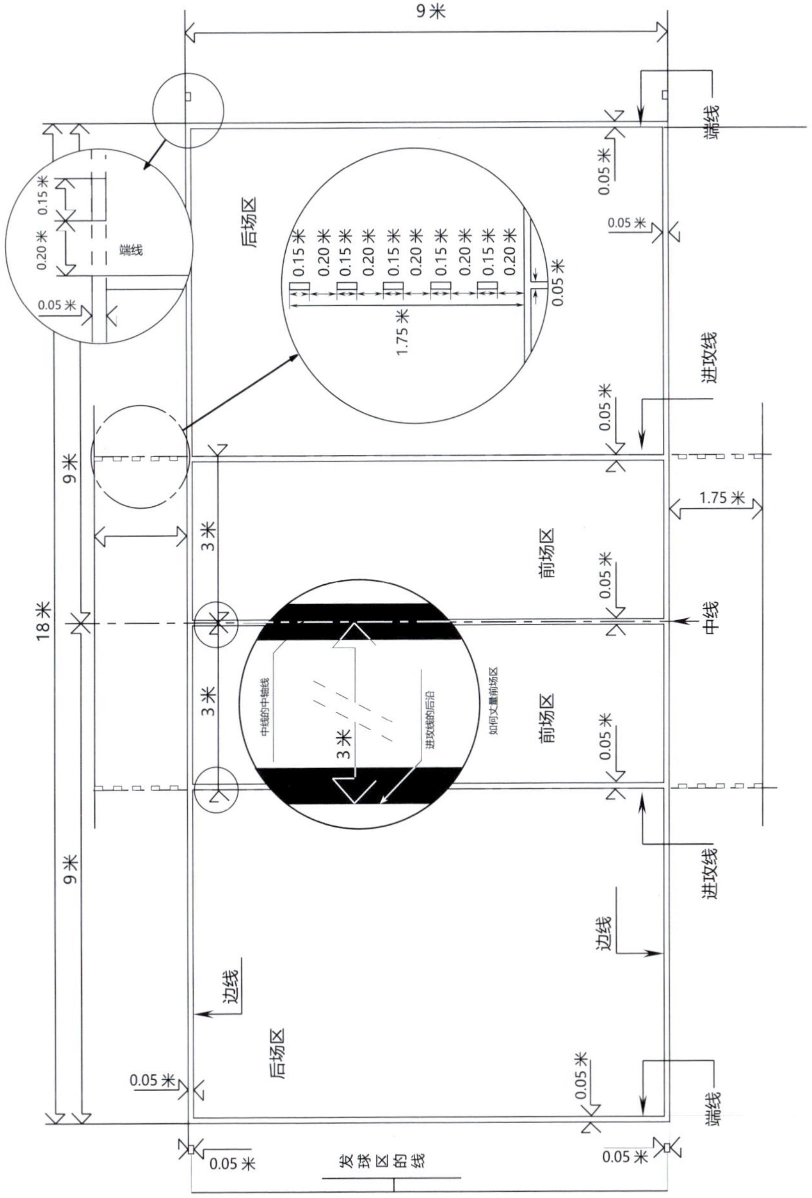

DIAGRAM 3: DESIGN OF THE NET

Relevant Rules: 2, 2.2, 2.3, 2.4, 2.5.1, 11.3.1, 11.3.2, 29.2.1.6

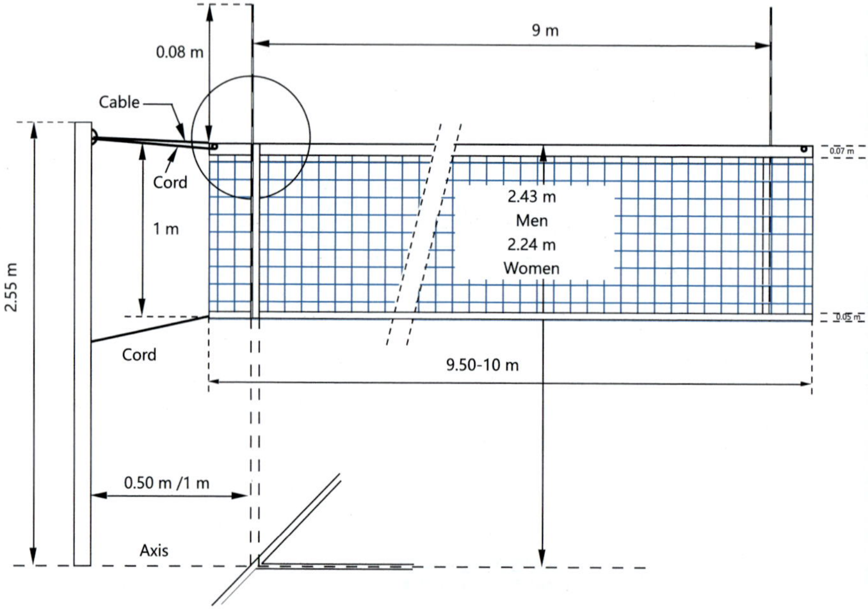

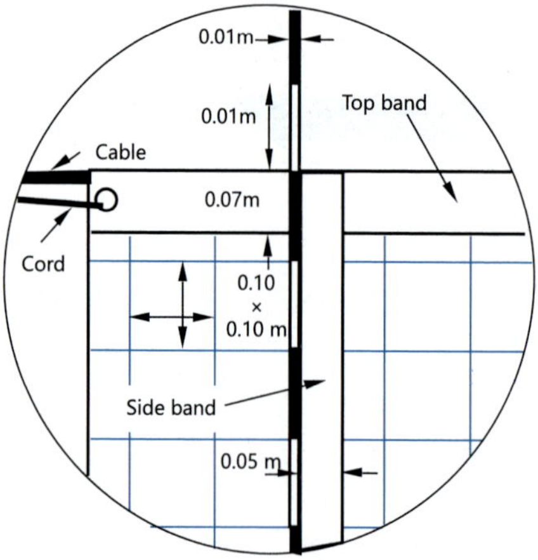

图 3　球网的规格

相关规则：2, 2.2, 2.3, 2.4, 2.5.1, 11.3.1, 11.3.2, 29.2.1.6

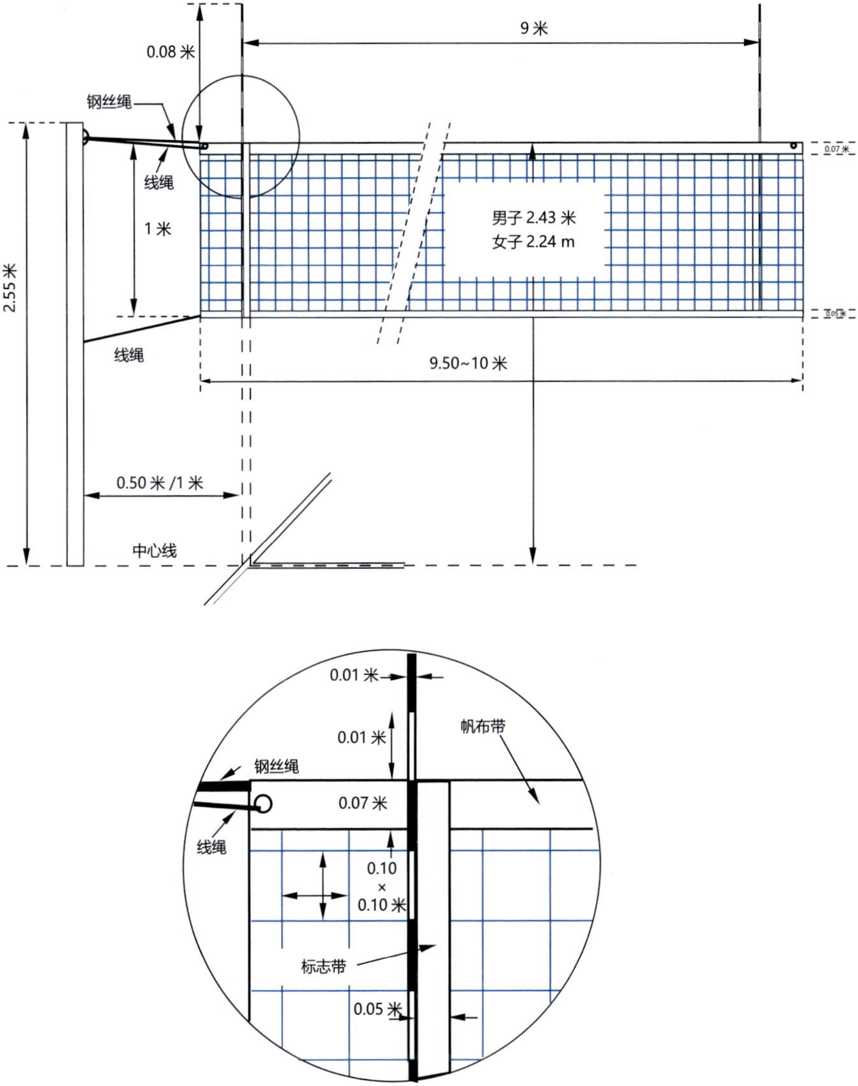

DIAGRAM 4: POSITION OF PLAYERS

Relevant Rules: 7.4, 7.4.3, 7.5, 23.3.2.3a, 24.3.2.2

Example A:

Determination of the positions between a front-row player and the corresponding back-row player

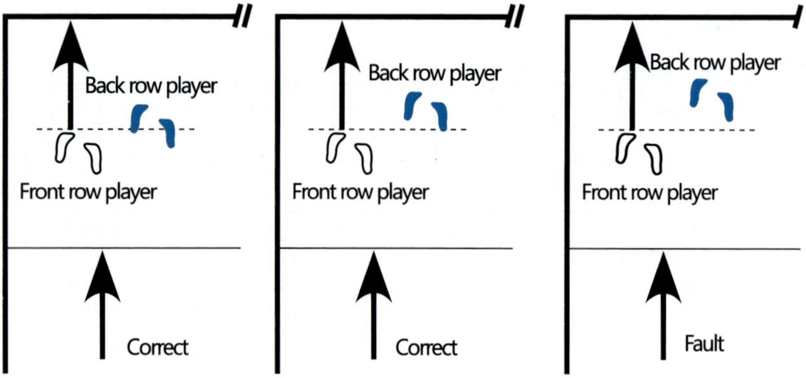

Example B:

Determination of the positions between players of the same row

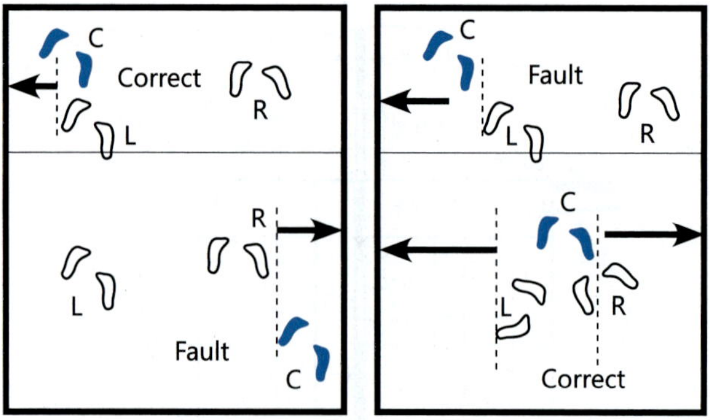

C (C) = Centre player

R (D) = Right player

L (G) = Left player

图 4：队员的位置

相关规则：7.4, 7.4.3, 7.5, 23.3.2.3a, 24.3.2.2

例 A:

前排队员与相应的后排队员位置关系

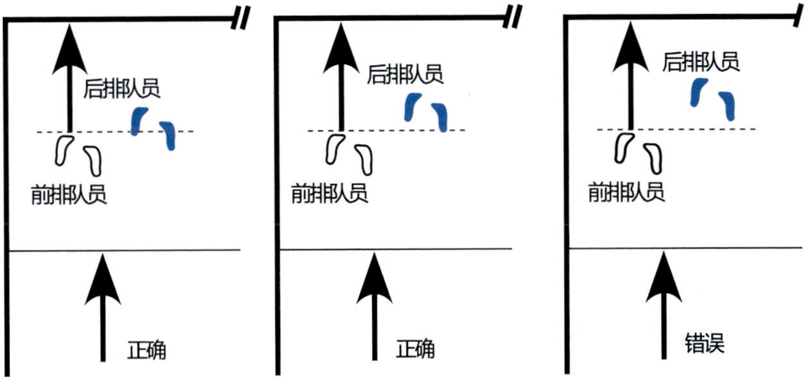

例 B:

同排队员位置关系

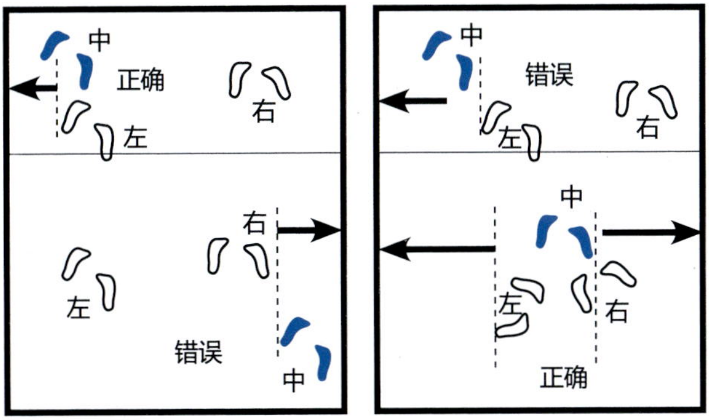

中 = 中间队员

右 = 右边队员

左 = 左边队员

DIAGRAM 5a: BALL CROSSING THE VERTICAL PLANE OF THE NET TO THE OPPONENT COURT

Relevant Rules: 2.4, 8.4.3, 8.4.4, 8.4.5, 10.1.1, 10.1.3, 24.3.2.7, 29.2.1.3, 29.2.1.7

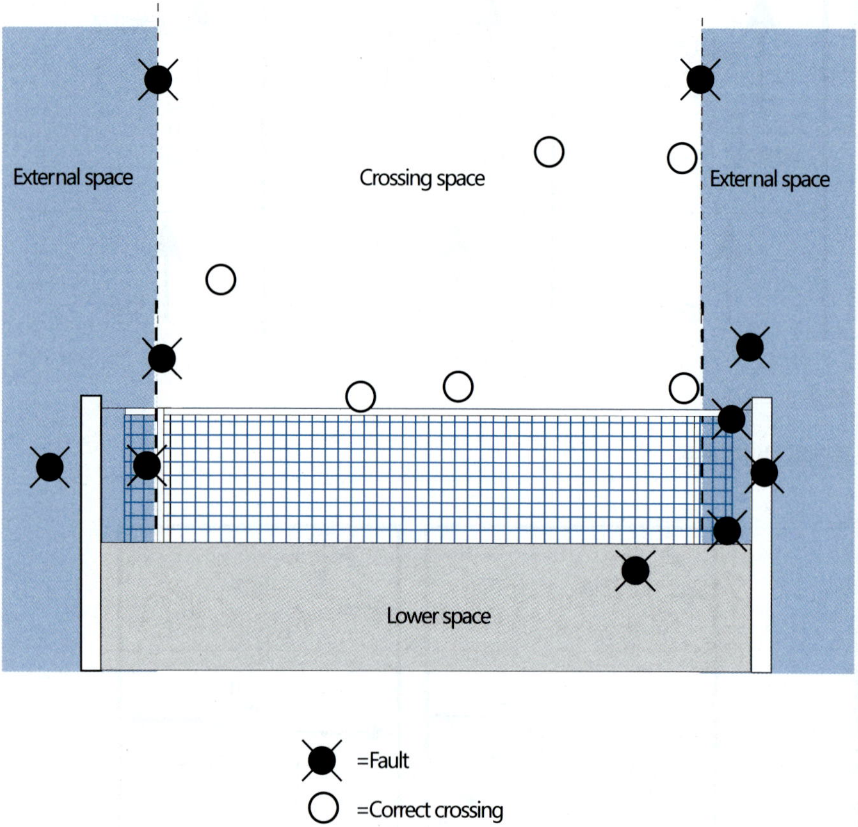

图 5a：球通过球网垂直平面进入对方场区

相关规则：2.4, 8.4.3, 8.4.4, 8.4.5, 10.1.1, 10.1.3, 24.3.2.7, 29.2.1.3, 29.2.1.7

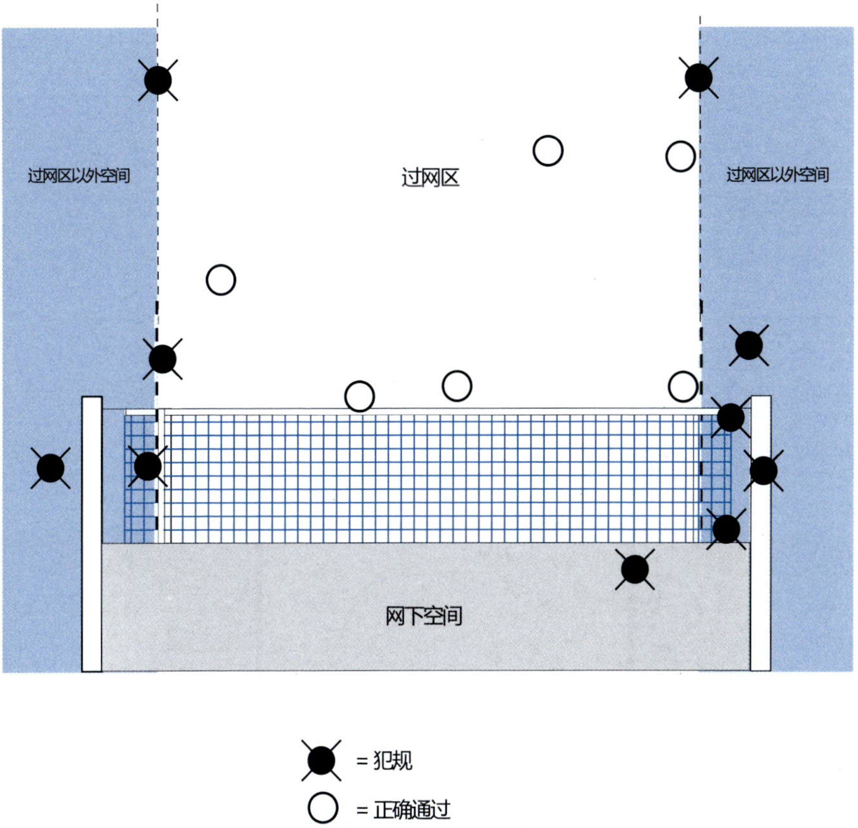

DIAGRAM 5b: BALL CROSSING THE VERTICAL PLANE OF THE NET TO THE OPPONENT FREE ZONE

Relevant Rules: 10.1.2, 10.1.2.2, 24.3.2.7

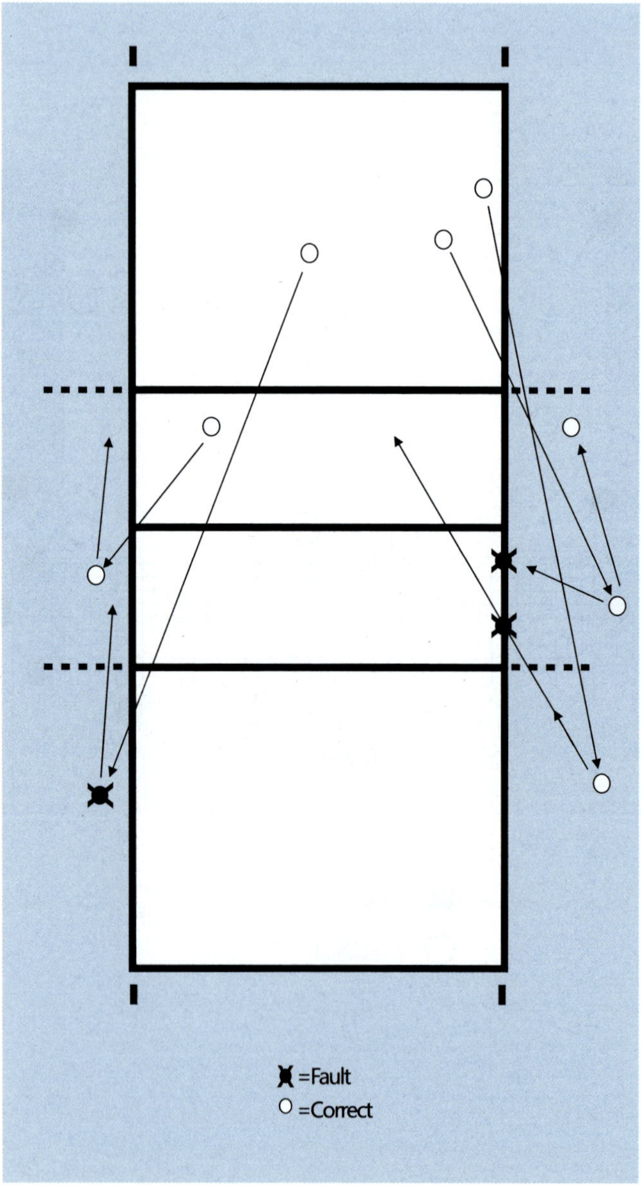

图 5b：球通过球网垂直平面进入对方无障碍区

相关规则：10.1.2, 10.1.2.2, 24.3.2.7

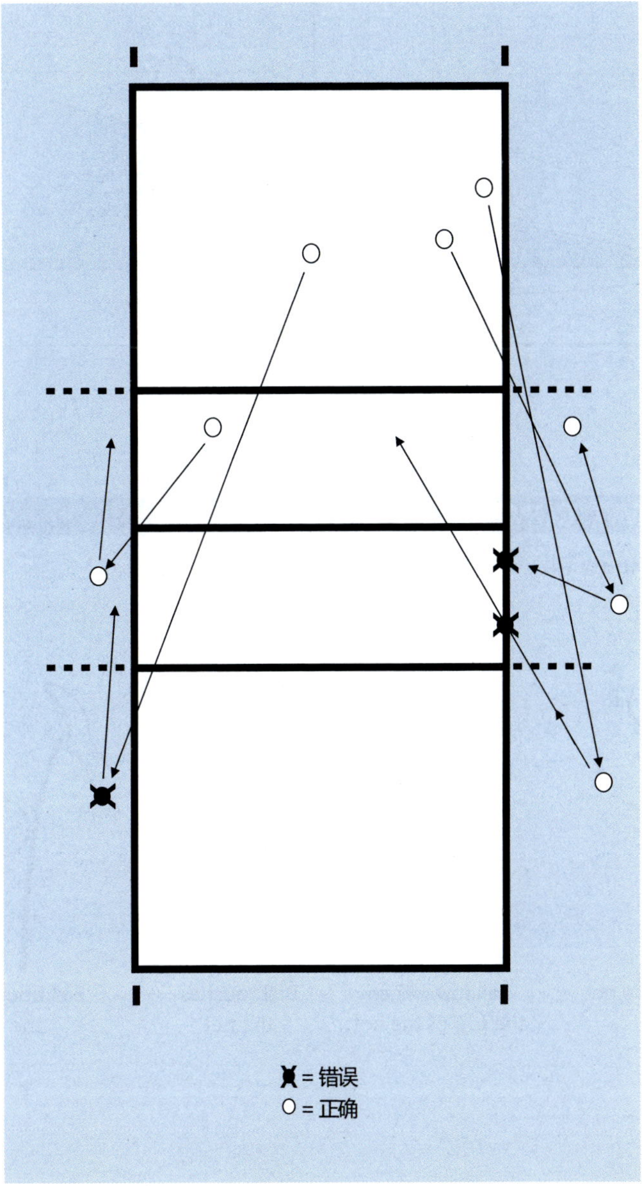

DIAGRAM 6: COLLECTIVE SCREEN

Relevant Rules: 12.5, 12.5.2, 23.3.2.3a

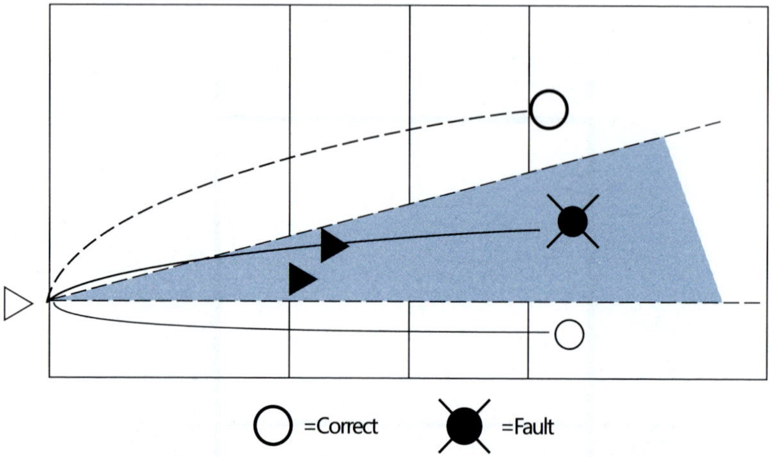

DIAGRAM 7: COMPLETED BLOCK

Relevant Rule: 14.1.3

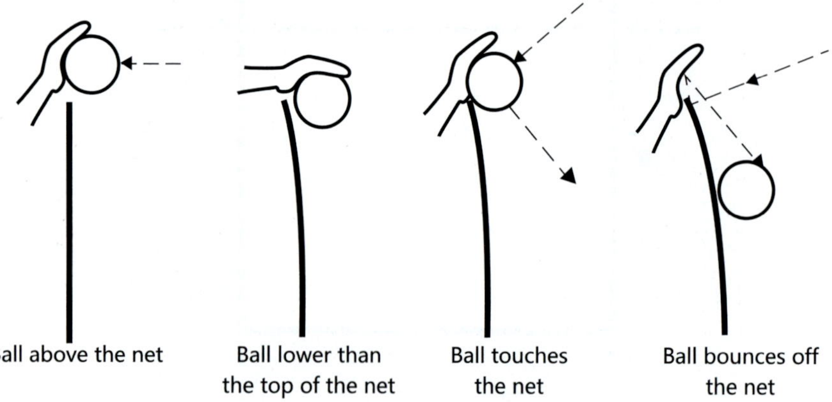

图 6：发球时的集体掩护

相关规则：12.5, 12.5.2, 23.3.2.3a

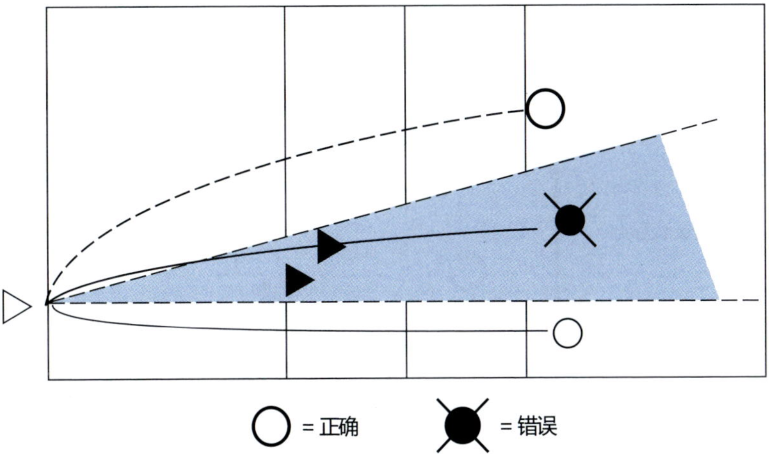

图 7：完成拦网

相关规则：14.1.3

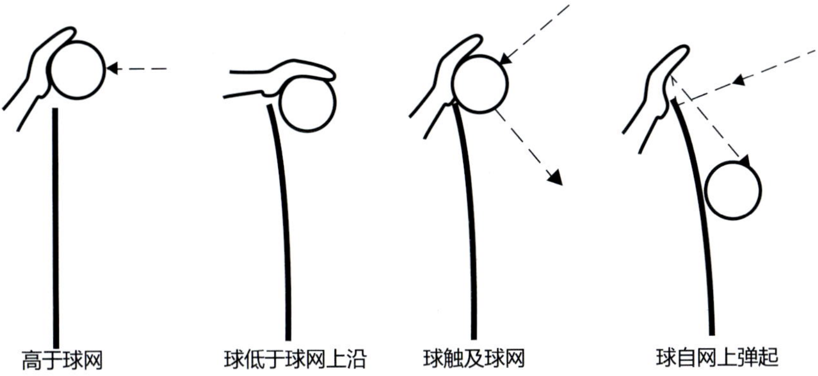

DIAGRAM 8: BACK ROW PLAYER' S ATTACK

Relevant Rules: 13.2.2, 13.2.3, 23.3.2.3d, 24.3.2.4

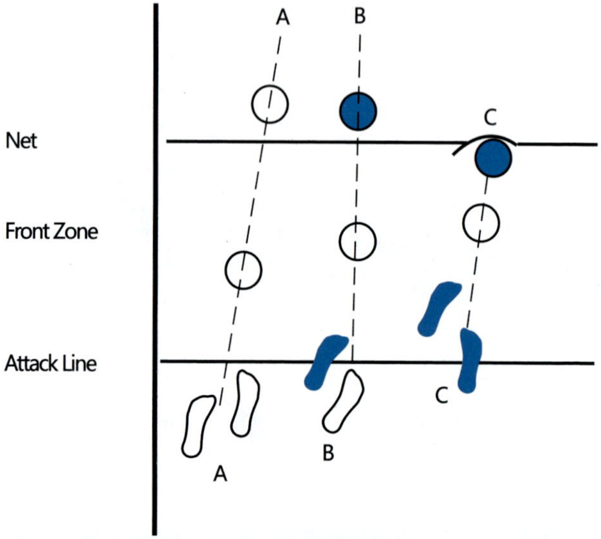

A = Correct

B, C = Fault

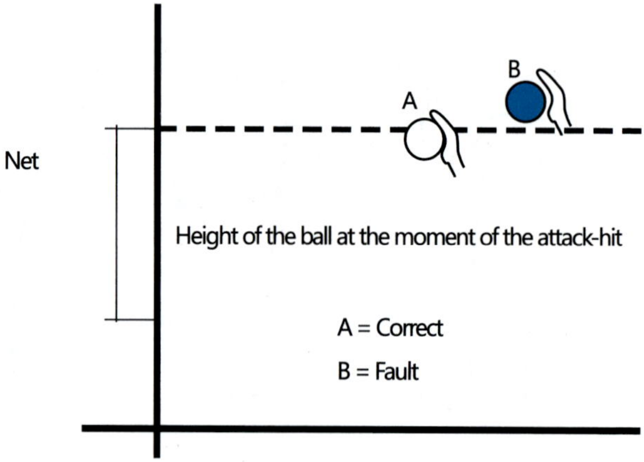

图 8：后排队员进攻性击球

相关规则：13.2.2, 13.2.3, 23.3.2.3d, 24.3.2.4

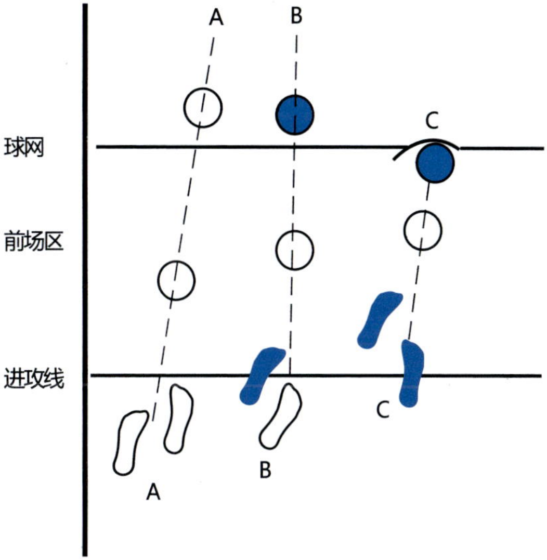

A = 正确

B, C = 错误

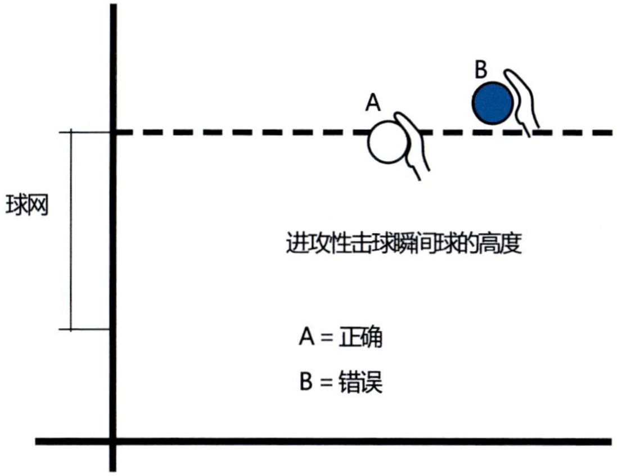

A = 正确

B = 错误

DIAGRAM 9: WARNINGS AND SANCTIONS SCALES AND THEIR CONSEQUENCES

Relevant Rules: 16.2, 21.3, 21.4.2

9a: MISCONDUCT WARNINGS AND SANCTIONS

CATEGORIES	OCCURRENCE	OFFENDER	SANCTION	CARDS	CONSEQUENCE
MINOR MISCONDUCT	Stage 1	Any member	Not considered as sanction	None	Prevention only
	Stage 2			Yellow	
	repetition any time				as below
RUDE CONDUCT	First	Any member	Penalty	Red	A point and service to the opponent
	Second	Same member	Expulsion	Red + Yellow jointly	Team member must go to the team's dressing room for the remainder of the set
	Third	Same member	Disqualification	Red + Yellow separately	Team member must go to the team's dressing room for the remainder of the match
OFFENSIVE CONDUCT	First	Any member	Expulsion	Red + Yellow jointly	Team member must go to the team's dressing room for the remainder of the set
	Second	Same member	Disqualification	Red + Yellow separately	Team member must go to the team's dressing room for the remainder of the match
AGGRESSION	First	Any member	Disqualification	Red + Yellow separately	Team member must go to the team's dressing room for the remainder of the match

9b: DELAY WARNING SYMBOLS AND SANCTIONS

CATEGORIES	OCCURRENCE	OFFENDER	DETERRENT or SANCTION	CARDS	CONSEQUENCE
DELAY	First	Any member of the team	Delay Warning	Hand signal No. 25 with Yellow card	Prevention – no penalty
	Second and subsequent	Any member of the team	Delay Penalty	Hand signal No. 25 with Red card	A point and service to the opponent

图 9：警告和处罚等级表及其后续结果

相关规则：16.2, 21.3, 21.4.2

9a：不良行为的警告和处罚

种类	发生次数	违反者	处罚	牌	结果
轻微的不良行为	形式一	任一成员	不进行判罚	无	警示和预防
	形式二			黄	
	任何重复				如下
粗鲁行为	第一次	任一成员	判罚	红	失一球并由对方发球
	第二次	同一成员	判罚出场	单手持红 + 黄	球队成员须前往球队更衣室至该局剩余比赛结束
	第三次	同一成员	取消比赛资格	双手分持红 + 黄	球队成员须前往球队更衣室至该场剩余比赛结束
冒犯行为	第一次	任一成员	判罚出场	单手持红 + 黄	球队成员须前往球队更衣室至该局剩余比赛结束
	第二次	同一成员	取消比赛资格	双手分持红 + 黄	球队成员须前往球队更衣室至该场剩余比赛结束
侵犯行为	第一次	任一成员	取消比赛资格	双手分持红 + 黄	球队成员须前往球队更衣室至该场剩余比赛结束

9b：延误处罚等级表

种类	发生次数	违反者	处罚	牌	结果
延误	第一次	同队的任一成员	延误警告	手势 25 黄牌	不予判罚防止重犯
	第二次（及其后的）	同队的任一成员	延误判罚	手势 25 红牌	对方得 1 分并发球

DIAGRAM 10: LOCATION OF REFEREEING TEAM AND THEIR ASSISTANTS

Relevant Rules: 3.3, 23.1, 24.1, 27.1, 28.1, 29.1

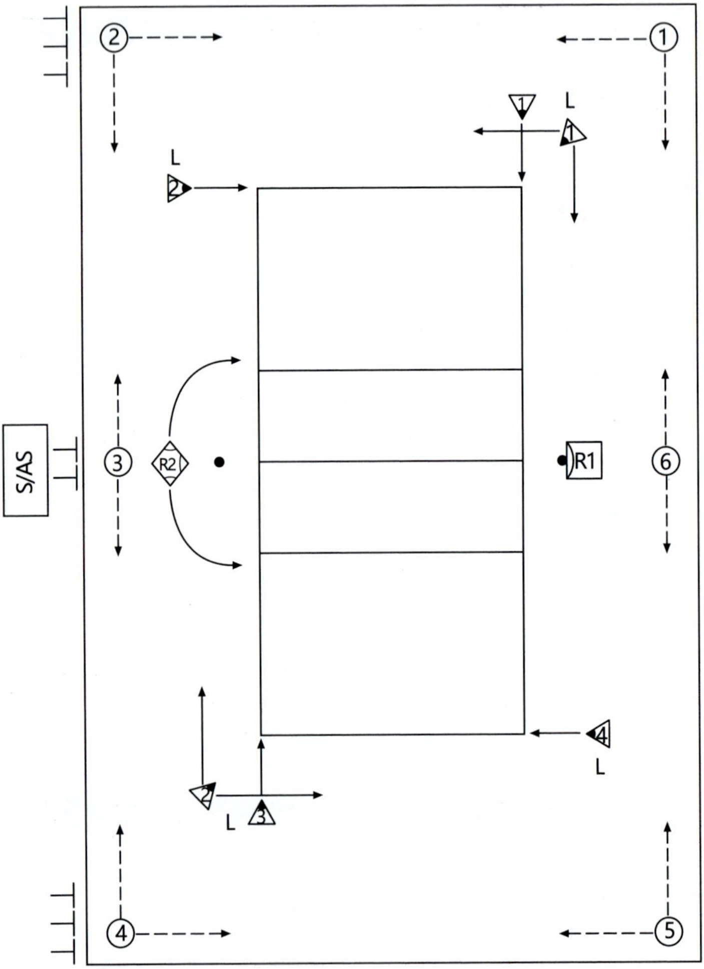

R1 = First Referee

R2 = Second Referee

S/AS = Scorer/Assistant Scorer

2 = Lines Judges (numbers 1-4 or 1-2)

4 = Ball Retrievers (numbers 1-6)

= Floor Moppers

图 10: 裁判员与辅助人员位置

相关规则：3.3, 23.1, 24.1, 27.1, 28.1, 29.1

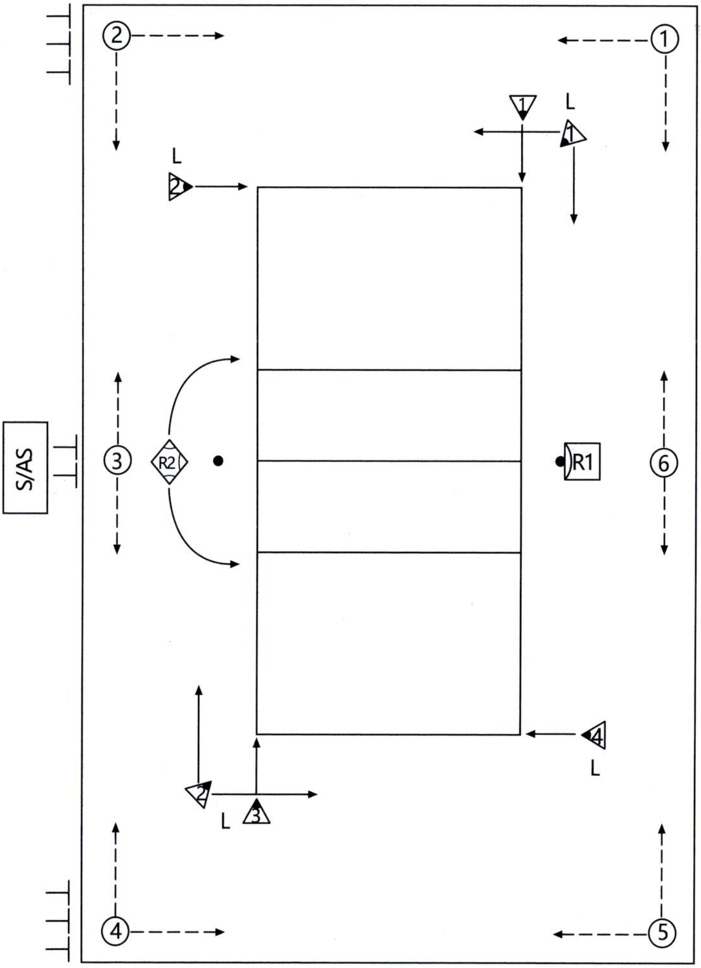

R1 = 第 1 裁判员

R2 = 第 2 裁判员

S/AS = 记录员 / 辅助记录员

2 = 司线员（1 号—4 号或 1 号—2 号）

④ = 捡球员（1 号—6 号）

⊣ = 擦地员

DIAGRAM 11: REFEREES' OFFICIAL HAND SIGNALS

Legend: Ⓕ Ⓢ Referee(s) who must show the signal according to their regular responsibilities

Ⓕ Ⓢ Referee(s) who show the signal in special situations

1 AUTHORISATION TO SERVE

Relevant Rules: 12.3, 22.2.1.1

Move the hand to indicate direction of service

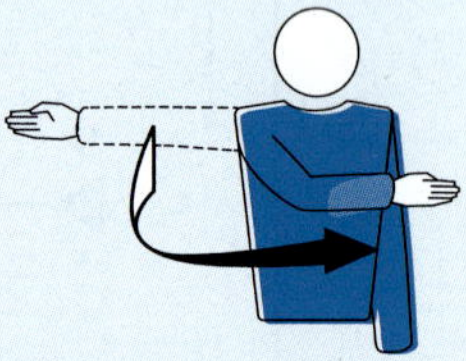

Ⓕ

2 TEAM TO SERVE

Relevant Rules: 22.2.3.1, 22.2.3.2, 22.2.3.4

Extend the arm to the side of team that will serve

Ⓕ Ⓢ

3 CHANGE OF COURTS

Relevant Rule: 18.2

Raise the forearms front and back and twist them around the body

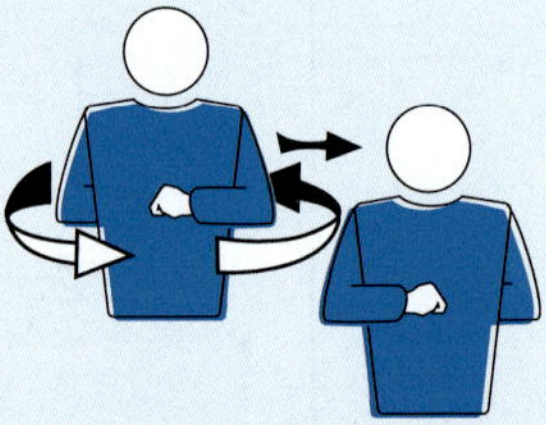

Ⓕ

4 TIME-OUT

Relevant Rule: 15.4.1

Place the palm of one hand over the fingers of the other, held vertically (forming a T) and then indicate the requesting team

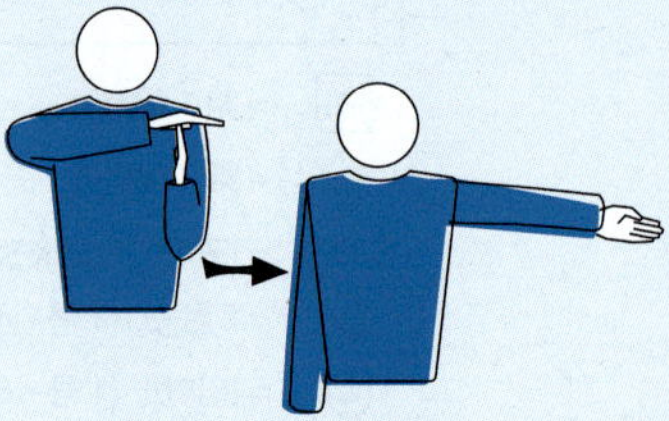

Ⓕ Ⓢ

图 11：裁判员手势

说明：第 1 裁判员 第 2 裁判员 依其常规职责必须出示手势的裁判员

第 1 裁判员 第 2 裁判员 在该特殊场景中出示手势的裁判员

1　允许发球

相关规则：12.3，22.2.1.1

挥动手臂，指出发球方向

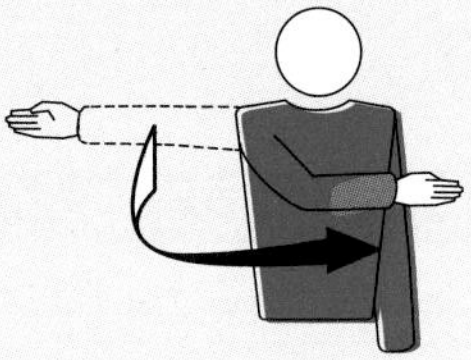

第 1 裁判员

2　发球队

相关规则：22.2.3.1，22.2.3.2，22.2.3.4

平举与发球队同侧的手臂

第 1 裁判员 第 2 裁判员

3　交换场区

相关规则：18.2

两臂屈肘，在身体前后绕旋

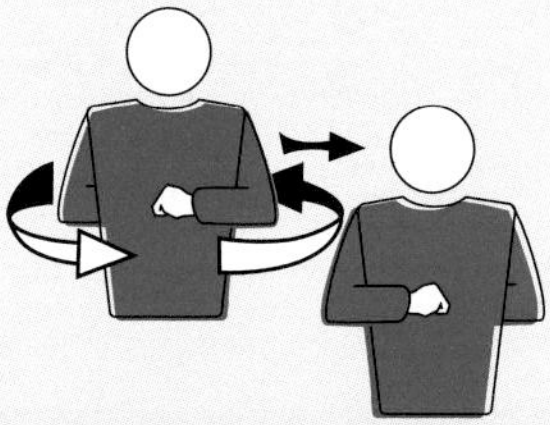

第 1 裁判员

4　暂停

相关规则：15.4.1

一臂屈肘抬起，手指向上；另一手掌垂直放在该手指尖上（形成“T”字型），然后指明提出请求的队

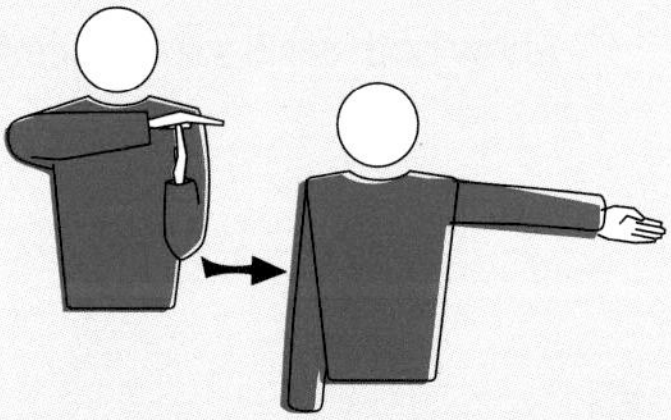

第 1 裁判员 第 2 裁判员

5 SUBSTITUTION

Relevant Rules: 15.5.1, 15.5.2, 15.8

Circular motion of the forearms around each other

F S

6a MISCONDUCT WARNING

Relevant Rules: 21.1, 21.6, 23.3.2.2

Show a yellow card for warning

F

6b MISCONDUCT PENALTY

Relevant Rules: 21.3.1, 21.6, 23.3.2.2

Show a red card for penalty

F

7 EXPULSION

Relevant Rules: 21.3.2, 21.6, 23.3.2.2

Show both cards jointly for expulsion

F

5 换人

相关规则：15.5.1，15.5.2，15.8

两臂屈肘在胸前绕环

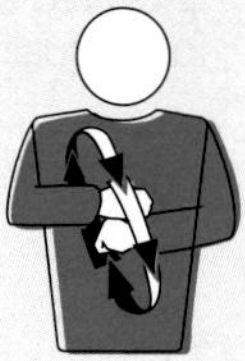

第 1 裁判员 第 2 裁判员

6a 不良行为的警告

相关规则：21.1，21.6，23.3.2.2

一手持黄牌举起

第 1 裁判员

6b 不良行为的判罚

相关规则：21.3.1，21.6，23.3.2.2

一手持红牌举起

第 1 裁判员

7 判罚出场

相关规则：21.3.2，21.6，23.3.2.2

一手持红牌和黄牌举起

第 1 裁判员

8 DISQUALIFICATION

Relevant Rules: 21.3.3, 21.6, 23.3.2.2

Show red and yellow cards separately for disqualification

F S

9 END OF SET (OR MATCH)

Relevant Rules: 6.2, 6.3

Cross the forearms in front of the chest, hands open

F S

10 BALL NOT TOSSED OR RELEASED AT THE SERVICE HIT

Relevant Rule: 12.4.1

Lift the extended arm, the palm of the hand facing upwards

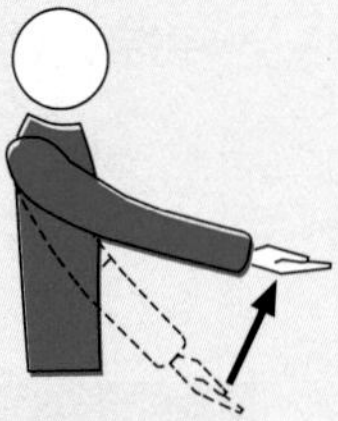

F

11 DELAY IN SERVICE

Relevant Rule: 12.4.4

Raise eight fingers, spread open

F

8　取消比赛资格

相关规则：21.3.3，21.6，23.3.2.2

双手分别持红、黄牌举起

第 1 裁判员　第 2 裁判员

9　一局（场）比赛结束

相关规则：6.2，6.3

两臂在胸前交叉，手伸开，掌心向内

第 1 裁判员　第 2 裁判员

10　发球时未抛起

相关规则：12.4.1

一臂慢慢举起，掌心向上

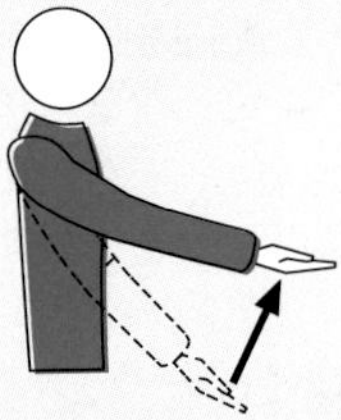

第 1 裁判员

11　发球延误

相关规则：12.4.4

举起 8 个手指并分开，掌心向前

第 1 裁判员

12 BLOCKING FAULT OR SCREENING

Relevant Rules: 12.5, 12.6.2.3, 14.6.3, 19.3.1.3, 23.3.2.3a, g, 24.3.2.4

Raise both arms vertically, palms forward

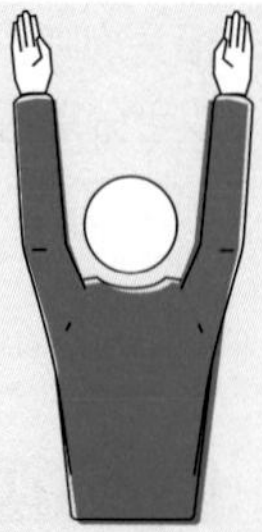

F S

13 POSITIONAL OR ROTATIONAL FAULT

Relevant Rules: 7.5, 7.7, 23.3.2.3a, 24.3.2.2

Make a circular motion with the forefinger

F S

14 BALL "IN"

Relevant Rule: 8.3

Point the arm and fingers toward the floor

F S

15 BALL "OUT"

Relevant Rules: 8.4.1, 8.4.2, 8.4.3, 8.4.4, 24.3.2.5, 24.3.2.7, 24.3.2.8

Raise the forearms vertically, hands open, palms towards the body

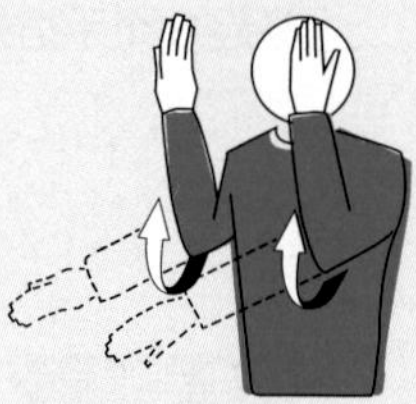

F S

12 发球掩护或拦网犯规

相关规则：12.5，12.6.2.3，14.6.3，19.3.1.3，23.3.2.3a，g，24.3.2.4

两臂上举，掌心向前

第 1 裁判员 第 2 裁判员

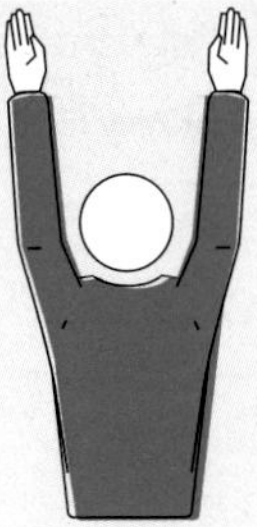

13 位置或轮转错误

相关规则：7.5，7.7，23.3.2.3a，24.3.2.2

一手食指在体前水平绕环

第 1 裁判员 第 2 裁判员

14 界内球

相关规则：8.3

手臂和手指指向地面

第 1 裁判员 第 2 裁判员

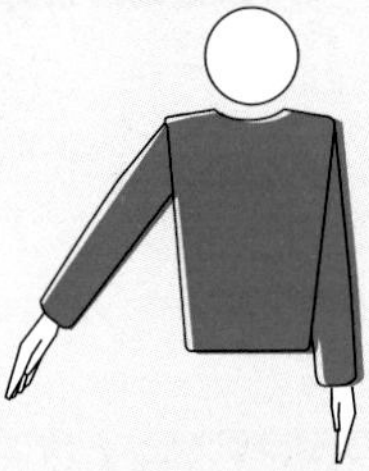

15 界外球

相关规则：8.4.1，8.4.2，8.4.3，8.4.4，24.3.2.5，24.3.2.7，24.3.2.8

两臂屈肘上举，掌心向后

第 1 裁判员 第 2 裁判员

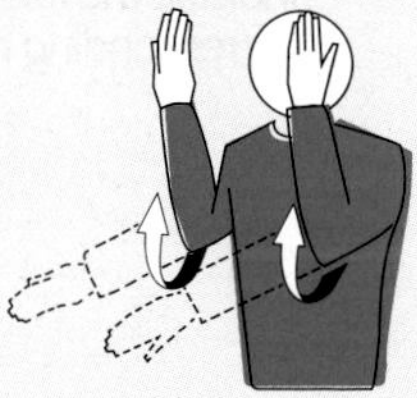

16 CATCH

Relevant Rules: 9.2.2, 9.3.3, 23.3.2.3b

Slowly lift the forearm, palm of the hand facing upwards

F

17 DOUBLE CONTACT

Relevant Rules: 9.3.4, 23.3.2.3b

Raise two fingers, spread open

F

18 FOUR HITS

Relevant Rules: 9.3.1, 23.3.2.3b

Raise four fingers, spread open

F

19 NET TOUCHED BY PLAYER - SERVED BALL TOUCHES THE NET BETWEEN THE ANTENNAE AND DOES NOT PASS THE VERTICAL PLANE OF THE NET

Relevant Rules: 11.4.4, 12.6.2.1

Indicate the relevant side of the net with the corresponding hand

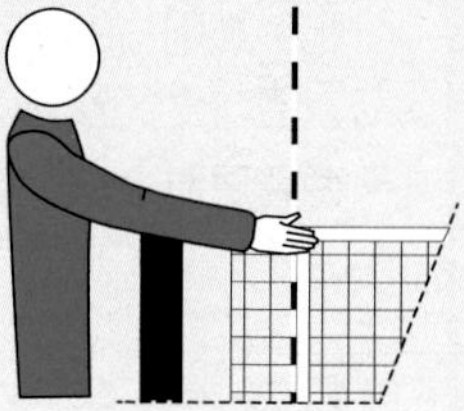

F S

16　持球

相关规则：9.2.2，9.3.3，23.3.2.3b

屈肘慢举前臂，掌心向上

第 1 裁判员

17　连击

相关规则：9.3.4，23.3.2.3b

竖起两个手指并分开，掌心向前

第 1 裁判员

18　4 次击球

相关规则：9.3.1，23.3.2.3b

竖起 4 个手指并分开，掌心向前

第 1 裁判员

19　队员触网和发球没有过网

相关规则：11.4.4，12.6.2.1

一手触犯规队一侧的球网

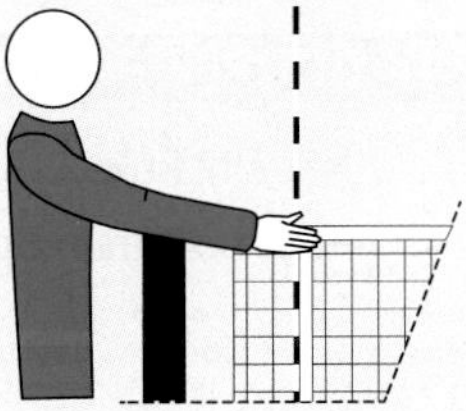

第 1 裁判员　第 2 裁判员

20 REACHING BEYOND THE NET

Relevant Rules: 11.4.1, 13.3.1, 14.3, 14.6.1, 23.3.2.3c

Place a hand above the net, palm facing downwards

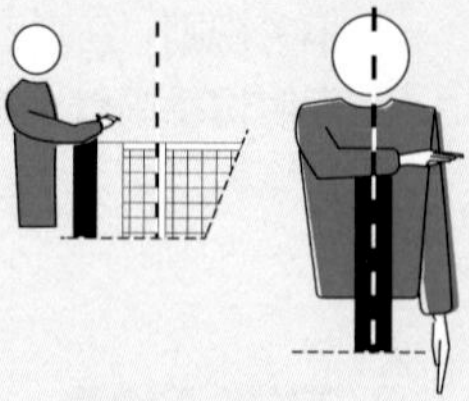

F

21 ATTACK HIT FAULT

Relevant Rules:
- by a back-row player, by a libero or on the opponent' s service:13.3.3, 13.3.4, 13.3.5, 23.3.2.3d, e, 24.3.2.4
- on an overhand finger pass by the libero in his/her front zone or its extension:13.3.6

Make a downward motion with the forearm, hand open

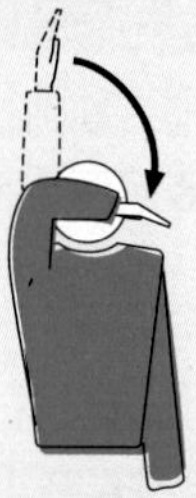

F S

22 PENETRATION INTO THE OPPONENT COURT BALL CROSSING THE LOWER SPACE OR THE SERVER TOUCHES THE COURT (END LINE) OR THE PLAYER STEPS OUTSIDE HIS/HER COURT AT THE MO MENT OF THE SERVICE HIT

Relevant Rules: 8.4.5, 11.2.2, 12.4.3, 23.3.2.3a, f, 24.3.2.1

Point to the center line or to the relevant line

F S

23 DOUBLE FAULT AND REPLAY

Relevant Rules: 6.1.2.2, 17.2, 22.2.3.4

Raise both thumbs vertically

F

20　过网犯规

相关规则：11.4.1，13.3.1，14.3，14.6.1，23.3.2.3c

前臂置于球网上空，掌心向下

第 1 裁判员

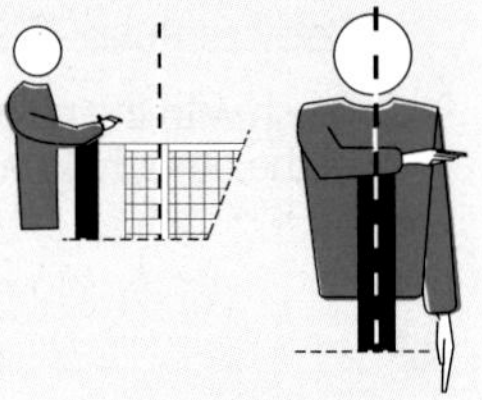

21　进攻性击球犯规

相关规则：

— 对后排队员、自由防守队员或对方发球：13.3.3，13.3.4，13.3.5，23.3.2.3d，e，24.3.2.4

— 对自由防守队员在前场区及其延长部分的上手传球：13.3.6

臂上举，前臂向下摆动，手掌张开

第 1 裁判员　第 2 裁判员

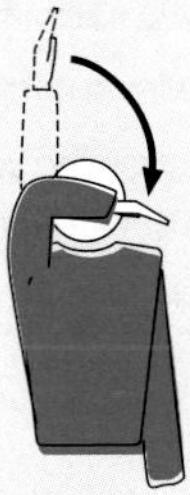

22　进入对方场区或球从网下通过或发球时脚的犯规或发球一刻队员不在场区之内

相关规则：8.4.5，11.2.2，12.4.3，23.3.2.3a，f，24.3.2.1

指向中线或相关的线

第 1 裁判员　第 2 裁判员

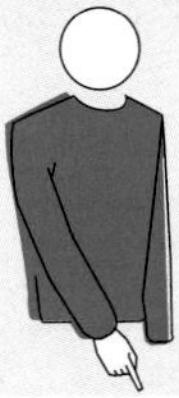

23　双方犯规和重新比赛

相关规则：6.1.2.2，17.2，22.2.3.4

两臂屈肘，竖起拇指

第 1 裁判员

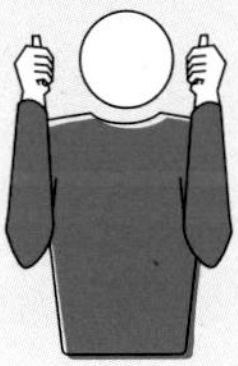

24 BALL TOUCHED

Relevant Rules: 23.3.2.3b, 24.2.2

Brush with the palm of one hand the fingers of the other, held vertically

F

25 DELAY WARNING / DELAY PENALTY

Relevant Rules: 15.11.3, 16.2.2, 16.2.3, 23.3.2.2

Cover the wrist with a yellow card (warning) and with a red card (penalty)

F

24　触手出界

相关规则：23.3.2.3b，24.2.2

用一手掌摩擦另一屈肘上举的指尖

第 1 裁判员

25　延误警告和判罚

相关规则：15.11.3，16.2.2，16.2.3，23.3.2.2

两臂屈肘上举，一手掌心向后，另一手持黄牌（警告）或红牌（判罚）贴靠其腕部

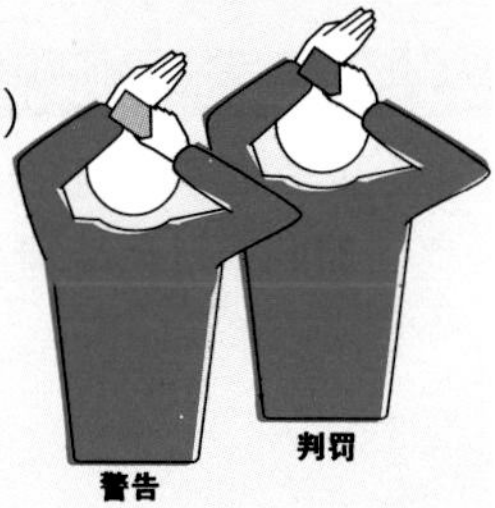

第 1 裁判员

DIAGRAM 12: LINE JUDGES' OFFICIAL FLAG SIGNALS

1 BALL "IN"

Relevant Rule: 8.3, 29.2.1.1

Point down with flag

L

2 BALL "OUT"

Relevant Rules: 8.4.1, 29.2.1.1

Raise flag vertically

L

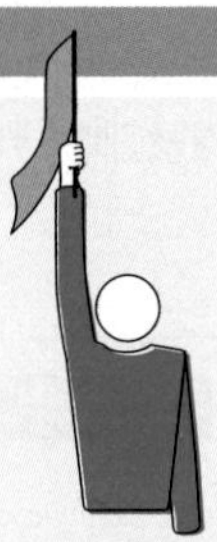

3 BALL TOUCHED

Relevant Rule: 29.2.1.2

Raise flag and touch the top with the palm of the free hand

L

4 CROSSING SPACE FAULTS, BALL TOUCHED AN OUTSIDE OBJECT, OR FOOT FAULT BY ANY PLAYER DURING SERVICE

Relevant Rules: 8.4.2, 8.4.3, 8.4.4, 12.4.3, 29.2.1.3, 29.2.1.4, 29.2.1.6, 29.2.1.7

Wave flag over the head and point to the antenna or the respective line

L

图 12：司线员旗示

1　界内球

相关规则：8.3，29.2.1.1

向下示旗

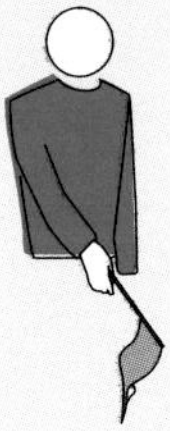

司线员

2　界外球

相关规则：8.4.1，29.2.1.1

向上示旗

司线员

3　触手出界

相关规则：29.2.1.2

一手举旗，另一手掌置于旗杆顶

司线员

4　发球时脚的犯规或球通过球网时的犯规、球触及场外物体的犯规等

相关规则：8.4.2，8.4.3，8.4.4，12.4.3，29.2.1.3，29.2.1.4，29.2.1.6，29.2.1.7

一手举旗绕环，另一手指标志杆、物体或相应的界线

司线员

5 JUDGEMENT IMPOSSIBLE

Raise and cross both arms and hands in front of the chest

L

5　无法判断

两臂胸前交叉

司线员

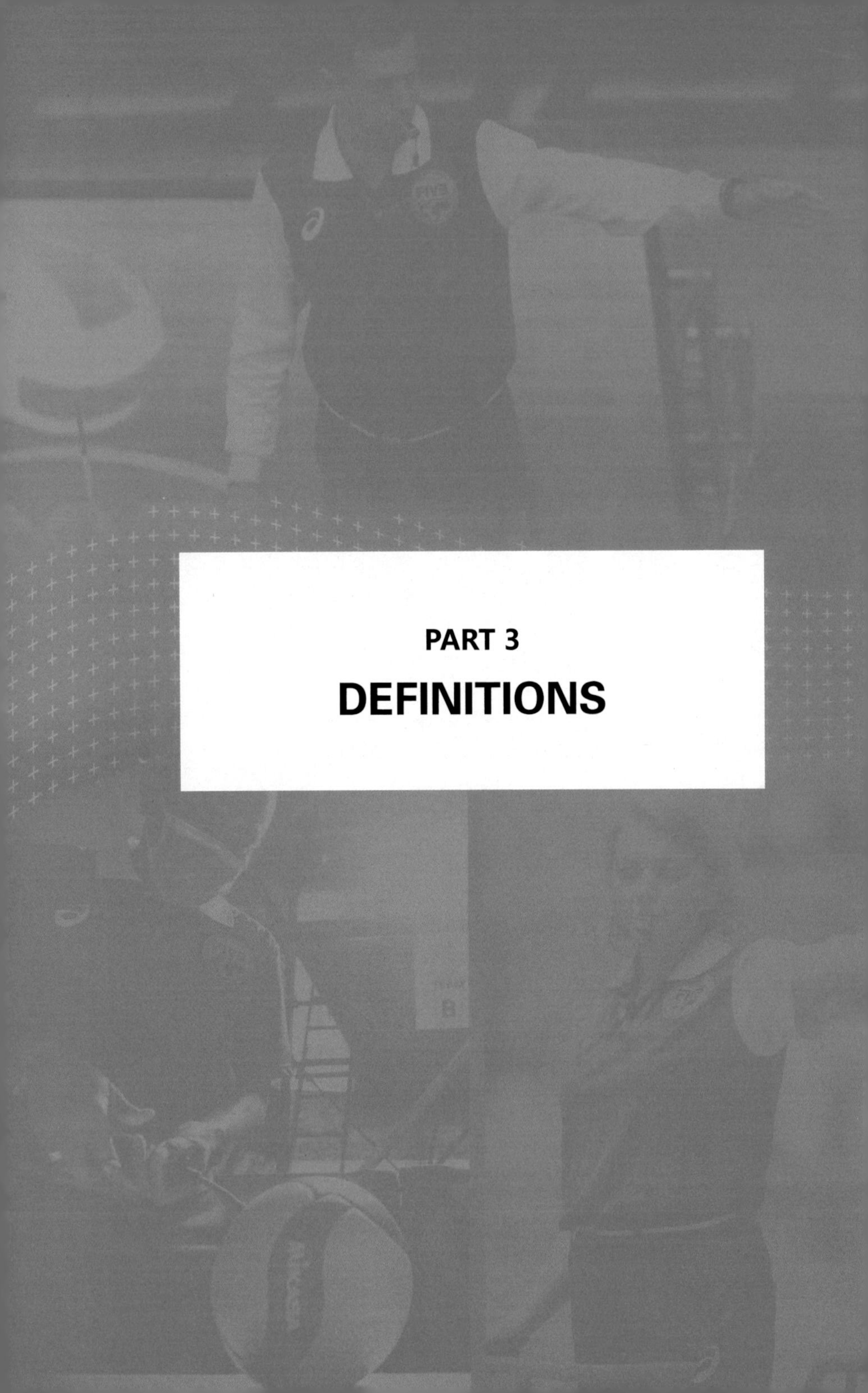

PART 3
DEFINITIONS

第三部分

定义

COMPETITION/ CONTROL AREA

The Competition/ Control Area is a corridor around the playing court and free zone, which includes all spaces up to the outer barriers or delimitation fence. See diagram/fig 1a.

ZONES

These are sections within the playing area (i.e. playing court and free zone) as defined for a specific purpose (or with special restrictions) within the rule text. These include: Front Zone, Service Zone, Substitution Zone, Free Zone, Back Zone, and Libero Replacement Zone.

AREAS

These are sections of the floor OUTSIDE the free zone, identified by the rules as having a specific function. These include: warm-up area.

LOWER SPACE

This is the space defined at its upper part by the bottom of the net and the cord joining it to the posts, at the sides by the posts, and the bottom by the playing surface.

CROSSING SPACE

The crossing space is defined by:

– The horizontal band at the top of the net
– The antennae and their extension
– The ceiling

The ball must cross to the opponent' s COURT through the crossing space.

EXTERNAL SPACE

The external space is in the vertical plane of the net outside of the crossing and lower spaces.

比赛控制区域

比赛控制区域是围绕比赛场区和无障碍区的走廊，包括广告牌或挡板以外的空间（见图 1）。

区

区是比赛场地中（比赛场区和无障碍区）的不同部分，在规则中赋予特殊定义（或特别限制）。区包括前场区、发球区、换人区、无障碍区、后场区和自由防守队员替换区。

区域

区域是无障碍区以外的地域，根据规则规定赋予其特殊功能。区域包括准备活动区。

网下空间

球网以下、地面以上、两根网柱之间的空间。

过网区

过网区的界限是：

— 球网的上沿；
— 两根标志杆及其延长线；
— 天花板。

球必须通过过网区进入对方场区。

延长空间

除过网区和网下空间之外的球网垂直空间。

SUBSTITUTION ZONE

This is the part of the free zone through which substitutions are carried out.

UNLESS BY AGREEMENT OF FIVB

This statement recognizes that while there are regulations on the standards and specification of equipment and facilities, there are occasions when special arrangements can be made by FIVB in order to promote the game of Volleyball or to test new conditions.

FIVB STANDARDS

The technical specifications or limits as defined by FIVB to the manufacturers of equipment.

FAULT

a) A playing action contrary to the rules.
b) A rule violation other than a playing action.

DRIBBLING

Dribbling means bouncing the ball (usually as a preparation to tossing and serving). Other preparatory actions could include (amongst others) moving the ball from hand to hand.

BALL RETRIEVERS AND QUICK MOPPERS

These are personnel whose job it is to maintain the flow of the game by rolling the ball to the server between rallies.

Quick moppers: are personnel whose job it is to keep the floor clean and dry if necessary, after each rally using small towels.

换人区

进行换人的那部分无障碍区。

国际排联（FIVB）特许

在特定的条件下，国际排联 (FIVB) 安排试用一些特殊器材、设备，目的在于改善比赛条件或推动排球运动发展。

国际排联（FIVB）标准

国际排联（FIVB）对生产厂家提出的技术规格和要求。

犯规

a) 违反规则的比赛行为；
b) 违反规则的非比赛行为。

摆弄球

球在手中或两手之间被倒动、旋转等（目的在于准备抛或发球）。

捡球员和快擦手

捡球员的职责是在比赛过程之间将球滚向或提供给发球队员以保证比赛流畅进行。

快擦手的职责是保持场地清洁和干燥，如有必要，在每一个比赛过程后使用小毛巾。

RALLY POINT

This is the system of scoring a point whenever a rally is won.

INTERVAL

The time between sets. The change of courts in the 5th (deciding) set is not to be regarded as an interval.

RE-DESIGNATION

This is the act by which a Libero, who cannot continue or is declared by the team "unable to play", has his/her role taken by any other player (except the regular replacement player) not on the court at the moment of the re-designation.

REPLACEMENT

This is the act by which a regular player leaves the court and either Libero (if more than one) takes his/her place. This can even include Libero for Libero exchanges. The regular player can then replace either Libero. There must be a completed rally between replacements involving any Libero.

INTERFERING

Any action which will create an advantage against the opponent team or any action which prevents an opponent from playing the ball.

O-2bis

An FIVB official form which registers players and team officials. It should be presented during the Preliminary Inquiry.

OUTSIDE OBJECT

An object or a person which while outside the playing court or close to the limit of the free playing space provides an obstruction to the flight of the ball. For example: overhead lights, the referee's chair, TV equipment, scorer's table, and net posts. Outside objects do not include the antennae since they are considered as the part of the net.

每球得分制

这是每胜 1 球都得 1 分的计分体系。

局间

两局之间的时间。第 5 局（决胜局）交换场区不能算作局间。

重新指定

当自由防守队员被他的球队宣布不能继续比赛时，可以由任何一名未在场上的队员替代（被自由防守队员替换过的原场上队员除外）。

自由防守队员替换

一名正常队员离场，其位置由任一自由防守队员替代（不止 1 名自由防守队员时）的过程。 自由防守队员替换可以在两名自由防守队员之间进行，也可以在其他队员与自由防守队员之间进行，但两次替换之间必须有完整的比赛过程。

干扰

对对方队员的行动和击球动作起到妨碍的行为。

O-2bis 表

国际排联填写参赛队员和球队官员的正式表格。此表格应在赛前进行运动队资格审查时提交。

场外物体

比赛场地之外或接近无障碍空间，并对球飞行造成障碍的物体或人，例如顶灯、 裁判椅、电视设备、记录台、网柱等。场外物体不包括标志杆，标志杆是球网的一部分。

SUBSTITUTION

This is the act by which one regular player leaves the court and another regular player takes his/her place.

FIRST HIT OF THE TEAM

There are four cases, when the playing action is considered first hit of the team:

– service reception
– receiving an attack of the opponent team
– playing the ball rebounding from own block
– playing the ball rebounding from opponent' s block

PROTOCOL

The series of events before the start of the match, including the toss, the warming-up session, presentation of the teams and referees described in the Specific Competition Handbook.

换人

一名队员离开比赛场地，并由另一名队员占据其位置的行为。

球队的第一次击球

以下四种情况中的比赛行为被视为球队的第一次击球：

— 接发球
— 接对方的进攻性击球
— 接本方拦网后弹回的球
— 接被对方拦回的球

赛前仪式

比赛开始前的一系列活动，包括：挑边、热身活动、根据技术手册的描述介绍运动队和裁判员。

FIVB™

fivb.com